A Wife For A Month by John Fletcher

John Fletcher was born in December, 1579 in Rye, Sussex. He was baptised on December 20th.

As can be imagined details of much of his life and career have not survived and, accordingly, only a very brief indication of his life and works can be given.

Young Fletcher appears at the very young age of eleven to have entered Corpus Christi College at Cambridge University in 1591. There are no records that he ever took a degree but there is some small evidence that he was being prepared for a career in the church.

However what is clear is that this was soon abandoned as he joined the stream of people who would leave University and decamp to the more bohemian life of commercial theatre in London.

The upbringing of the now teenage Fletcher and his seven siblings now passed to his paternal uncle, the poet and minor official Giles Fletcher. Giles, who had the patronage of the Earl of Essex may have been a liability rather than an advantage to the young Fletcher. With Essex involved in the failed rebellion against Elizabeth Giles was also tainted.

By 1606 John Fletcher appears to have equipped himself with the talents to become a playwright. Initially this appears to have been for the Children of the Queen's Revels, then performing at the Blackfriars Theatre.

Fletcher's early career was marked by one significant failure; The Faithful Shepherdess, his adaptation of Giovanni Battista Guarini's Il Pastor Fido, which was performed by the Blackfriars Children in 1608.

By 1609, however, he had found his stride. With his collaborator John Beaumont, he wrote Philaster, which became a hit for the King's Men and began a profitable association between Fletcher and that company. Philaster appears also to have begun a trend for tragicomedy.

By the middle of the 1610s, Fletcher's plays had achieved a popularity that rivalled Shakespeare's and cemented the pre-eminence of the King's Men in Jacobean London. After his frequent early collaborator John Beaumont's early death in 1616, Fletcher continued working, both singly and in collaboration, until his own death in 1625. By that time, he had produced, or had been credited with, close to fifty plays.

Index of Contents

A WIFE FOR A MONTH

DRAMATIS PERSONAE
MEN
Alphonso, King of Naples, elder Brother to Frederick
Frederick, unnatural and libidinous Brother to Alphonso, and usurper of his Kingdom
Sorano, a Lord, Brother to Evanthe, Frederick's wicked instrument
Valerio, a noble young Lord, servant to Evanthe
Camillo   }
Cleanthes   } Three honest Court Lords
Menallo   }
Rugio, an honest Lord, friend to Alphonso
Marco, a Frier, Alphonso's friend
Podramo, a necessary creature to Sorano
Cupid   } with other Masquers
Graces }
Tonie, King Frederick's Knavish fool
Castruccio, Captain of the Cittadel, an honest man
Citizens
Lawyer
Physician
Captain
Cut-purse
Fool
Attendants
WOMEN
Queen, Wife to Frederick, a vertuous Lady
Evanthe, Sister to Sorano, the chaste Wife of Valerio, or a Wife for a Month
Cassandra, an old Bawd, Waiting-woman to Evanthe
Ladies
City-Wives

THE SCENE: Naples.

You are wellcome Gentlemen, and would our Feast
Were so well season'd, to please every Guest;
Ingenuous appetites, I hope we shall,
And their examples may prevail in all.
Our noble friend, who writ this, bid me say,
He had rather dress, upon a Triumph day,
My Lord Mayors Feast, and make him Sawces too,
Sawce for each several mouth, nay further go,
He had rather build up those invincible Pyes
And Castle Custards that affright all eyes,
Nay eat 'em all and their Artillery,
Than dress for such a curious company
One single dish; yet he has pleas'd ye too,
And you've confest he knew well what to do;
Be hungry as you were wont to be, and bring,
Sharp stomachs to the stories he shall sing,
And he dare yet, he saies, prepare a Table
Shall make you say, well drest, and he well able.

ACTUS PRIMUS

SCÆNA PRIMA

Enter **KING FREDERICK**, **SORANO**, **VALERIO**, **CAMILLO**, **CLEANTHES**, **MENALLO** and **ATTENDANTS**.

SORANO
Will your Grace speak?

FREDERICK
Let me alone, Sorano,
Although my thoughts seem sad, they are welcome to me.

SORANO
You know I am private as your secret wishes,
Ready to fling my soul upon your service,
E're your command be on't.

FREDERICK
Bid those depart.

SORANO
You must retire my Lords.

CAMILLO

What new design is hammering in his head now?

CLEANTHES
Let's pray heartily
None of our heads meet with it, my Wife's old,
That's all my comfort.

MENALLO
Mine's ugly, that I am sure on,
And I think honest too, 'twould make me start else.

CAMILLO
Mine's troubled in the Country with a Feaver,
And some few infirmities else; he looks again,
Come let's retire, certain 'tis some she-business,
This new Lord is imployed.

VALERIO
I'le not be far off, because I doubt the cause.

[Exit.

FREDERICK
Are they all gone?

SORANO
All but your faithful Servant.

FREDERICK
I would tell thee,
But 'tis a thing thou canst not like.

SORANO
Pray ye speak it, is it my head? I have it ready for ye, Sir:
Is't any action in my power? my wit?
I care not of what nature, nor what follows.

FREDERICK
I am in love.

SORANO
That's the least thing of a thousand,
The easiest to atchieve.

FREDERICK
But with whom, Sorano?

SORANO

With whom you please, you must not be deny'd, Sir.

FREDERICK
Say it be with one of thy Kinswomen.

SORANO
Say withal,
I shall more love your Grace, I shall more honour ye,
And would I had enough to serve your pleasure.

FREDERICK
Why 'tis thy Sister then, the fair Evanthe,
I'le be plain with thee.

SORANO
I'le be as plain with you, Sir,
She brought not her perfections to the world,
To lock them in a case, or hang 'em by her,
The use is all she breeds 'em for, she is yours, Sir.

FREDERICK
Dost thou mean seriously?

SORANO
I mean my Sister,
And if I had a dozen more, they were all yours:
Some Aunts I have, they have been handsome Women,
My Mother's dead indeed, and some few Cousins
That are now shooting up, we shall see shortly.

FREDERICK
No, 'tis Evanthe.

SORANO
I have sent my man unto her,
Upon some business to come presently
Hither, she shall come; your Grace dare speak unto her?
Large golden promises, and sweet language, Sir,
You know what they work, she is a compleat Courtier,
Besides I'le set in.

FREDERICK
She waits upon my Queen,
What jealousie and anger may arise,
Incensing her?

SORANO
You have a good sweet Lady,

A Woman of so even and still a temper,
She knows not anger; say she were a fury,
I had thought you had been absolute, the great King,
The fountain of all honours, plays and pleasures,
Your will and your commands unbounded also;
Go get a pair of Beads and learn to pray, Sir.

[Enter **SERVANT**.

SERVANT
My Lord, your servant stayes.

SORANO
Bid him come hither, and bring the Lady with him.

FREDERICK
I will woo her,
And either lose my self, or win her favour.

SORANO
She is coming in.

FREDERICK
Thy eyes shoot through the door,
They are so piercing, that the beams they dart
Give new light to the room.

[Enter **PODRAMO** and **EVANTHE**.

EVANTHE
Whither dost thou go?
This is the Kings side, and his private lodgings,
What business have I here?

PODRAMO
My Lord sent for ye.

EVANTHE
His lodgings are below, you are mistaken,
We left them at the stair-foot.

PODRAMO
Good sweet Madam.

EVANTHE
I am no Counsellor, nor important Sutor,
Nor have no private business through these Chambers,
To seek him this way, o' my life thou art drunk,

Or worse than drunk, hir'd to convey me hither
To some base end; now I look on thee better,
Thou hast a bawdy face, and I abhor thee,
A beastly bawdy face, I'le go no further.

SORANO
Nay shrink not back, indeed you shall good Sister,
Why do you blush? the good King will not hurt ye,
He honours ye, and loves ye.

EVANTHE
Is this the business?

SORANO
Yes, and the best you ever will arrive at if you be wise.

EVANTHE
My Father was no bawd, Sir,
Nor of that worshipful stock as I remember.

SORANO
You are a Fool.
Evan, You are that I shame to tell ye.

FREDERICK
Gentle Evanthe.

EVANTHE
The gracious Queen, Sir,
Is well and merry, Heaven be thanked for it,
And as I think she waits you in the Garden.

FREDERICK
Let her wait there, I talk not of her Garden,
I talk of thee sweet Flower.

EVANTHE
Your Grace is pleasant,
To mistake a Nettle for a Rose.

FREDERICK
No Rose, nor Lilly, nor no glorious Hyacinth
Are of that sweetness, whiteness, tenderness,
Softness, and satisfying blessedness
As my Evanthe.

EVANTHE
Your Grace speaks very feelingly,

I would not be a handsome wench in your way, Sir,
For a new Gown.

FREDERICK
Thou art all handsomness,
Nature will be asham'd to frame another
Now thou art made, thou hast rob'd her of her cunning:
Each several part about thee is a beauty.

SORANO
Do you hear this Sister?

EVANTHE
Yes, unworthy Brother, but all this will not do.

FREDERICK
But love Evanthe.
Thou shalt have more than words, wealth, ease, and honours,
My tender Wench.

EVANTHE
Be tender of my credit,
And I shall love you, Sir, and I shall honour ye.

FREDERICK
I love thee to enjoy thee, my Evantbe,
To give thee the content of love.

EVANTHE
Hold, hold, Sir, ye are too fleet,
I have some business this way, your Grace can ne'r content.

SORANO
You stubborn toy.

EVANTHE
Good my Lord Bawd I thank ye.

FREDERICK
Thou shalt not go believe me, sweet Evanthe,
So high I will advance thee for this favour,
So rich and potent I will raise thy fortune,
And thy friends mighty.

EVANTHE
Good your Grace be patient,
I shall make the worst honourable wench that ever was,
Shame your discretion, and your choice.

FREDERICK
Thou shalt not.

EVANTHE
Shall I be rich do you say, and glorious,
And shine above the rest, and scorn all beauties,
And mighty in command?

FREDERICK
Thou shalt be any thing.

EVANTHE
Let me be honest too, and then I'le thank ye.
Have you not such a title to bestow too?
If I prove otherwise, I would know but this, Sir;
Can all the power you have or all the riches,
But tye mens tongues up from discoursing of me,
Their eyes from gazing at my glorious folly,
Time that shall come, from wondering at my impudence,
And they that read my wanton life from curses?
Can you do this? have ye this Magick in ye?
This is not in your power, though you be a Prince, Sir,
No more than evil is in holy Angels,
Nor I, I hope: get wantonness confirm'd
By Act of Parliament an honesty,
And so receiv'd by all, I'le hearken to ye.
Heaven guide your Grace.

FREDERICK
Evanthe, stay a little,
I'le no more wantonness, I'le marry thee.

EVANTHE
What shall the Queen do?

FREDERICK
I'le be divorced from her.

EVANTHE
Can you tell why? what has she done against ye?
Has she contrived a Treason 'gainst your Person?
Abus'd your bed? does disobedience urge ye?

FREDERICK
That's all one, 'tis my will.

EVANTHE

'Tis a most wicked one,
A most absurd one, and will show a Monster;
I had rather be a Whore, and with less sin,
To your present lust, than Queen to your injustice.
Yours is no love, Faith and Religion fly it,
Nor has no taste of fair affection in it,
Some Hellish flame abuses your fair body,
And Hellish furies blow it; look behind ye,
Divorce ye from a Woman of her beauty,
Of her integrity, her piety?
Her love to you, to all that honours ye,
Her chaste and vertuous love, are these fit causes?
What will you do to me, when I have cloy'd ye?
You may find time out in eternity,
Deceit and violence in heavenly Justice,
Life in the grave, and death among the blessed,
Ere stain or brack in her sweet reputation.

SORANO

You have fool'd enough, be wise now, and a woman,
You have shew'd a modesty sufficient,
If not too much for Court.

EVANTHE

You have shew'd an impudence,
A more experienc'd bawd would blush and shake at;
You will make my kindred mighty.

FREDERICK

Prethee hear me.

EVANTHE

I do Sir, and I count it a great offer.

FREDERICK

Any of thine.

EVANTHE

'Tis like enough you may clap honour on them,
But how 'twill sit, and how men will adore it,
Is still the question. I'le tell you what they'l say, Sir,
What the report will be, and 'twill be true too,
And it must needs be comfort to your Master,
These are the issues of her impudence:
I'le tell your Grace, so dear I hold the Queen,
So dear that honour that she nurs'd me up in,
I would first take to me, for my lust, a Moor,
One of your Gally-slaves, that cold and hunger,

Decrepit misery, had made a mock-man,
Than be your Queen.

FREDERICK
You are bravely resolute.

EVANTHE
I had rather be a Leper, and be shun'd,
And dye by pieces, rot into my grave,
Leaving no memory behind to know me,
Than be a high Whore to eternity.

FREDERICK
You have another Gamester I perceive by ye,
You durst not slight me else.

SORANO
I'le find him out,
Though he lye next thy heart hid, I'le discover him,
And ye proud peat, I'le make you curse your insolence.

VALERIO
Tongue of an Angel, and the truth of Heaven,
How am I blest!

[Exit **VALERIO**.

SORANO
Podramo go in hast
To my Sisters Gentlewoman, you know her well,
And bid her send her Mistris presently
The lesser Cabinet she keeps her Letters in,
And such like toyes, and bring it to me instantly. Away.

PODRAMO
I am gone.

[Exit.

[Enter the **QUEEN** with two **LADIES**.

SORANO
The Queen.

FREDERICK
Let's quit the place, she may grow jealous.

[Exit **FREDERICK** and **SORANO**.

QUEEN
So suddenly departed! what's the reason?
Does my approach displease his Grace? are my eyes
So hateful to him? or my conversation
Infected, that he flies me? Fair Evanthe,
Are you there? then I see his shame.

EVANTHE
'Tis true, Madam,
'Thas pleas'd his goodness to be pleasant with me.

QUEEN
'Tis strange to find thy modesty in this place,
Does the King offer fair? does thy face take him?
Ne'r blush Evanthe, 'tis a very sweet one,
Does he rain gold, and precious promises
Into thy lap? will he advance thy fortunes?
Shalt thou be mighty, Wench?

EVANTHE
Never mock, Madam;
'Tis rather on your part to be lamented,
At least reveng'd, I can be mighty Lady,
And glorious too, glorious and great, as you are.

QUEEN
He will Marry thee?

EVANTHE
Who would not be a Queen, Madam?

QUEEN
'Tis true Evanthe, 'tis a brave ambition,
A golden dream, that may delude a good mind,
What shall become of me?

EVANTHE
You must learn to pray,
Your age and honour will become a Nunnery.

QUEEN
Wilt thou remember me?

[Weeps.

EVANTHE
She weeps. Sweet Lady

Upon my knees I ask your sacred pardon,
For my rude boldness: and know, my sweet Mistris,
If e're there were ambition in Evanthe,
It was and is to do you faithful duties;
'Tis true I have been tempted by the King,
And with no few and potent charms, to wrong ye,
To violate the chaste joyes of your bed;
And those not taking hold, to usurp your state;
But she that has been bred up under ye,
And daily fed upon your vertuous precepts,
Still growing strong by example of your goodness,
Having no errant motion from obedience,
Flyes from these vanities, as meer illusions;
And arm'd with honesty, defies all promises.
In token of this truth, I lay my life down
Under your sacred foot, to do you service.

QUEEN
Rise my true friend, thou vertuous bud of beauty,
Thou Virgins honour, sweetly blow and flourish,
And that rude nipping wind, that seeks to blast thee,
Or taint thy root, be curst to all posterity;
To my protection from this hour I take ye,
Yes, and the King shall know—

EVANTHE
Give his heat way, Madam,
And 'twill go out again, he may forget all.

[Exeunt.

[Enter **CAMILLO**, **CLEANTHES** and **MENALLO**.

CAMILLO
What have we to do with the times? we cannot cure 'em.
Let 'em go on, when they are swoln with Surfeits
They'l burst and stink, then all the world shall smell 'em.

CLEANTHES
A man may live a bawd, and be an honest man.

MENALLO
Yes, and a wise man too, 'tis a vertuous calling.

CAMILLO
To his own Wife especially, or to his Sister,
The nearer to his own bloud, still the honester;
There want such honest men, would we had more of 'em.

MENALLO
To be a villain is no such rude matter.

CAMILLO
No, if he be a neat one, and a perfect,
Art makes all excellent: what is it, Gentlemen,
In a good cause to kill a dozen Coxcombs,
That blunt rude fellows call good Patriots?
Nothing, nor ne'r look'd after.

MENALLO
'Tis e'en as much, as easie too, as honest, and as clear,
To ravish Matrons, and, deflower coy Wenches,
But here they are so willing, 'tis a complement.

CLEANTHES
To pull down Churches with pretension
To build 'em fairer, may be done with honour,
And all this time believe no gods.

CAMILLO
I think so, 'tis faith enough if they name 'em in their angers,
Or on their rotten Tombs ingrave an Angel;
Well, brave Alphonso, how happy had we been,
If thou had'st raign'd!

MENALLO
Would I had his Disease,
Tyed like a Leprosie to my posterity,
So he were right again.

CLEANTHES
What is his Malady?

CAMILLO
Nothing but sad and silent melancholy,
Laden with griefs and thoughts, no man knows why neither;
The good Brandino Father to the Princess
Used all the art and industry that might be,
To free Alphonso from this dull calamity,
And seat him in his rule, he was his eldest
And noblest too, had not fair nature stopt in him,
For which cause this was chosen to inherit,
Frederick the younger.

CLEANTHES
Does he use his Brother

With that respect and honour that befits him?

CAMILLO
He is kept privately, as they pretend,
To give more ease and comfort to his sickness;
But he has honest servants, the grave Rugio,
And Fryar Marco, that wait upon his Person.
And in a Monastery he lives.

MENALLO
'Tis full of sadness,
To see him when he comes to his Fathers Tomb,
As once a day that is his Pilgrimage,
Whilst in Devotion, the Quire sings an Anthem:
How piously he kneels, and like a Virgin
That some cross Fate had cozen'd of her Love,
Weeps till the stubborn Marble sweats with pity,
And to his groans the whole Quire bears a Chorus.

[Enter **FREDERICK**, **SORANO**, with the **CABINET** and **PODRAMO**.

CAMILLO
So do I too. The King with his Contrivers,
This is no place for us.

[Exeunt **LORDS**.

FREDERICK
This is a jewel,
Lay it aside, what paper's that?

PODRAMO
A Letter,
But 'tis a womans, Sir, I know by the hand,
And the false Orthography, they write old Saxon.

FREDERICK
May be her ghostly Mother's that instructs her.

SORANO
No, 'tis a Cousins, and came up with a great Cake.

FREDERICK
What's that?

SORANO
A pair of Gloves the Dutchess gave her,
For so the outside says.

FREDERICK
That other paper?

SORANO
A Charm for the tooth-ach, here's nothing but Saints and Crosses.

FREDERICK
Look in that Box, methinks that should hold secrets.

PODRAMO
'Tis Paint, and curls of Hair, she begins to exercise.
A glass of Water too, I would fain taste it,
But I am wickedly afraid 'twill silence me,
Never a Conduit-Pipe to convey this water.

SORANO
These are all Rings, Deaths-heads, and such Memento's
Her Grandmother, and worm-eaten Aunts left to her,
To tell her what her Beauty must arrive at.

FREDERICK
That, that.

PODRAMO
They are written songs, Sir, to provoke young Ladies;
Lord, here's a Prayer-Book, how these agree!
Here's a strange union.

SORANO
Ever by a surfeit you have a julep set to cool the Patient.

FREDERICK
Those, those.

SORANO
They are Verses to the blest Evanthe.

FREDERICK
Those may discover,
Read them out, Sorano.

SORANO
To the blest Evanthe.

Let those complain that feel Loves cruelty.
And in sad legends write their woes,

With Roses gently has corected me,
My War is without rage or blows:
My Mistriss eyes shine fair on my desires,
And hope springs up enflam'd with her new fires.

No more an Exile will I dwell,
With folded arms, and sighs all day,
Reckoning the torments of my Hell,
And flinging my sweet joys away:
I am call'd home again to quiet peace,
My Mistriss smiles, and all my sorrows cease.

Yet what is living in her Eye?
Or being blest with her sweet tongue,
If these no other joys imply?
A golden Give, a pleasing wrong:
To be your own but one poor Month, I'd give
My Youth, my Fortune, and then leave to live.

FREDERICK
This is my Rival, that I knew the hand now.

SORANO
I know it, I have seen it, 'tis Valerio's,
That hopeful Gentlemans, that was brought up with ye,
And by your charge, nourish'd and fed
At the same Table, with the same allowance.

FREDERICK
And all this courtesie to ruine me?
Cross my desires? 'had better have fed humblier,
And stood at greater distance from my fury:
Go for him quickly, find him instantly,
Whilst my impatient heart swells high with choler;
Better have lov'd despair, and safer kiss'd her.

[Exit **LORDS**.

[Enter **EVANTHE** and **CASSANDRA**.

EVANTHE
Thou old weak fool, dost thou know to what end,
To what betraying end he got this Casket?
Durst thou deliver him without my Ring,
Or a Command from mine own mouth, that Cabinet
That holds my heart? you unconsiderate Ass,
You brainless Ideot.

CASSANDRA

I saw you go with him,
At the first word commit your Person to him,
And make no scruple, he is your Brothers Gentleman,
And for any thing I know, an honest man;
And might not I upon the same security deliver him a Box?

EVANTHE

A Bottle-head.

FREDERICK

You shall have cause to chafe, as I will handle it.

EVANTHE

I had rather thou hadst delivered me to Pirats,
Betray'd me to uncurable diseases,
Hung up my Picture in a Market-place,
And sold me to wild Bawds.

CASSANDRA

As I take it, Madam,
Your maiden-head lies not in that Cabinet,
You have a Closer, and you keep the Key too,
Why are you vex'd thus?

EVANTHE

I could curse thee wickedly,
And wish thee more deformed than Age can make thee,
Perpetual hunger, and no teeth to satisfie it,
Wait on thee still, nor sleep be found to ease it;
Those hands that gave the Casket, may the Palsie
For ever make unuseful, even to feed thee:
Long winters, that thy Bones may turn to Isicles,
No Hell can thaw again, inhabit by thee.
Is thy Care like thy Body, all one crookedness?
How scurvily thou cryest now! like a Drunkard,
I'll have as pure tears from a dirty spout;
Do, swear thou didst this ignorantly, swear it,
Swear and be damn'd, thou half Witch.

CASSANDRA

These are fine words, well Madam, Madam.

EVANTHE

'Tis not well, thou mummy,
'Tis impudently, basely done, thou durty—

FREDERICK

Has your young sanctity done railing, Madam,
Against your innocent 'Squire? do you see this Sonnet,
This loving Script? do you know from whence it came too?

EVANTHE
I do, and dare avouch it pure, and honest.

FREDERICK
You have private Visitants, my noble Lady,
That in sweet numbers court your goodly Vertues,
And to the height of adoration.

EVANTHE
Well, Sir,
There's neither Heresie nor Treason in it.

FREDERICK
A Prince may beg at the door, whilst these feast with ye;
A favour or a grace, from such as I am,

[Enter **VALERIO** and **PODRAMO**.

Course common things.
You are welcome; Pray come near Sir,
Do you know this paper?

VALERIO
I am betray'd; I do, Sir,
'Tis mine, my hand and heart, if I dye for her,
I am thy Martyr, Love, and time shall honour me.

CASSANDRA
You sawcy Sir, that came in my Ladies name,
For her gilt Cabinet, you cheating Sir too,
You scurvy Usher, with as scurvy legs,
And a worse face, thou poor base hanging holder,
How durst thou come to me with a lye in thy mouth?
An impudent lye?

PODRAMO
Hollow, good Gill, you hobble.

CASSANDRA
A stinking lye, more stinking than the teller,
To play the pilfering Knave? there have been Rascals
Brought up to fetch and carry, like your Worship,
That have been hang'd for less, whipt they are daily,
And if the Law will do me right—

PODRAMO

What then old Maggot?

CASSANDRA

Thy Mother was carted younger; I'll have thy hide,
Thy mangy hide, embroider'd with a dog-whip,
As it is now with potent Pox, and thicker.

FREDERICK

Peace good Antiquity, I'll have your Bones else
Ground into Gunpowder to shoot at Cats with;
One word more, and I'll blanch thee like an almond,
There's no such cure for the she-falling sickness
As the powder of a dryed Bawds Skin, be silent.
You are very prodigal of your service here, Sir,
Of your life more it seems.

VALERIO

I repent neither,
Because your Grace shall understand it comes
From the best part of Love, my pure affection,
And kindled with chaste flame, I will not flye from it,
If it be errour to desire to marry,
And marry her that sanctity would dote on,
I have done amiss, if it be a Treason
To graft my soul to Vertue, and to grow there,
To love the tree that bears such happiness;
Conceive me, Sir, this fruit was ne'r forbidden;
Nay, to desire to taste too, I am Traytor;
Had you but plants enough of this blest Tree, Sir,
Set round about your Court, to beautifie it,
Deaths twice so many, to dismay the approachers,
The ground would scarce yield Graves to noble Lovers.

FREDERICK

'Tis well maintain'd, you wish and pray to fortune,
Here in your Sonnet, and she has heard your prayers,
So much you dote upon your own undoing,
But one Month to enjoy her as your Wife,
Though at the expiring of that time you dye for't.

VALERIO

I could wish many, many Ages, Sir,
To grow as old as Time in her embraces,
If Heaven would grant it, and you smile upon it;
But if my choice were two hours, and then perish,
I would not pull my heart back.

FREDERICK

You have your wish,
To morrow I will see you nobly married,
Your Month take out in all content and pleasure;
The first day of the following Month you dye for't;
Kneel not, not all your Prayers can divert me;
Now mark your sentence, mark it, scornful Lady,
If when Valerio's dead, within twelve hours,
For that's your latest time, you find not out
Another Husband on the same condition
To marry you again, you dye your self too.

EVANTHE

Now you are merciful, I thank your Grace.

FREDERICK

If when you are married, you but seek to 'scape
Out of the Kingdom, you, or she, or both,
Or to infect mens minds with hot commotions,
You dye both instantly; will you love me now, Lady?
My tale will now be heard, but now I scorn ye.

[Exit.

[Manent **VALERIO** and **EVANTHE**.

EVANTHE

Is our fair love, our honest, our entire,
Come to this hazard?

VALERIO

'Tis a noble one, and I am much in love with malice for it,
Envy could not have studied me a way,
Nor fortune pointed out a path to Honour,
Straighter and nobler, if she had her eyes;
When I have once enjoy'd my sweet Evanthe,
And blest my Youth with her most dear embraces,
I have done my journey here, my day is out,
All that the World has else is foolery,
Labour, and loss of time; what should I live for?
Think but mans life a Month, and we are happy.
I would not have my joys grow old for any thing;
A Paradise, as thou art, my Evanthe,
Is only made to wonder at a little,
Enough for human eyes, and then to wander from.
Come, do not weep, sweet, you dishonour me,
Your tears and griefs but question my ability,

Whether I dare dye; Do you love intirely?

EVANTHE
You know I do.

VALERIO
Then grudge not my felicity.

EVANTHE
I'll to the Queen.

VALERIO
Do any thing that's honest,
But if you sue to him, in Death I hate you.

[Exeunt.

SCÆNA PRIMA

Enter **CAMILLO**, **CLEANTHES** and **MENALLO**.

CAMILLO
Was there ever heard of such a Marriage?

MENALLO
Marriage and Hanging go by destiny,
'Tis the old Proverb, now they come together.

CLEANTHES
But a Month married, then to lose his life for't?
I would have a long Month sure, that pays the Souldiers.

[Enter **TONY** with Urinal.

CAMILLO
Or get all the Almanacks burnt, that were a rare trick,
And have no Month remembred. How now Tony?
Whose water are you casting?

TONY
A sick Gentlemans,
Is very sick, much troubled with the Stone,
He should not live above a Month, by his Urine,
About St. David's Day it will go hard with him,

He will then be troubled with a pain in his Neck too.

MENALLO
A pestilent fool; when wilt thou marry, Tony?

TONY
When I mean to be hang'd, & 'tis the surer contract.

CLEANTHES
What think you of this Marriage of Valerio's?

TONY
They have given him a hot Custard, and mean to burn his mouth with it; had I known he had been given to dye honourably, I would have helpt him to a Wench, a rare one, should have kill'd him in three weeks, and sav'd the sentence.

CAMILLO
There be them would have spared ten days of that too.

TONY
It may be so, you have Women of all Vertues:
There be some Guns that I could bring him too,
Some mortar-pieces that are plac'd i'th' Suburbs,
Would tear him into quarters in two hours,
There be also of the race of the old Cockatrices,
That would dispatch him with once looking on him.

MENALLO
What Month wouldst thou chuse, Tony, if thou hadst the like Fortune?

TONY
I would chuse a mull'd sack-month, to comfort my Belly, for sure my Back would ake for't, and at the months end I would be most dismally drunk, & scorn the gallows.

MENALLO
I would chuse March, for I would come in like a Lion.

TONY
But you'd go out like a Lamb when you went to hanging.

CAMILLO
I would take April, take the sweet o'th' year,
And kiss my Wench upon the tender flowrets,
Tumble on every Green, and as the Birds sung,
Embrace, and melt away my Soul in pleasure.

TONY
You would go a Maying gayly to the Gallows.

CLEANTHES

Prithee tell us some news.

TONY

I'll tell ye all I know,
You may be honest, and poor fools, as I am,
And blow your fingers ends.

CAMILLO

That's no news, Fool.

TONY

You may be knaves then when you please, stark knaves,
And build fair houses, but your heirs shall have none of 'em.

MENALLO

These are undoubted.

TONY

Truth is not worth the hearing,
I'll tell you news then; There was a drunken Saylor,
That got a Mermaid with child as she went a milking,
And now she sues him in the Bawdy-Court for it,
The infant-Monster is brought up in Fish-Street.

CAMILLO

I, this is something.

TONY

I'll tell you more, there was a Fish taken,
A monstrous Fish, with a sword by his side, a long sword,
A Pike in's Neck, and a Gun in's Nose, a huge Gun,
And letters of Mart in's mouth, from the Duke of Florence.

CLEANTHES

This is a monstrous lye.

TONY

I do confess it:
Do you think I would tell you truths, that dare not hear 'em?
You are honest things, we Courtiers scorn to converse with.

[Exit.

CAMILLO

A plaguey fool: but let's consider, Gentlemen,
Why the Queen strives not to oppose this sentence,

The Kingdoms honour suffers in this cruelty.

MENALLO
No doubt the Queen, though she be vertuous,
Winks at the Marriage, for by that only means
The Kings flame lessens to the youthful Lady,
If not goes out; within this Month, I doubt not,
She hopes to rock asleep his anger also;
Shall we go see the preparation?
'Tis time, for strangers come to view the wonder.

CAMILLO
Come, let's away, send my friends happier weddings.

[Exeunt.

[Enter **QUEEN** and **EVANTHE**.

QUEEN
You shall be merry, come, I'll have it so,
Can there be any nature so unnoble?
Or anger so inhumane to pursue this?

EVANTHE
I fear there is.

QUEEN
Your fears are poor and foolish,
Though he be hasty, and his anger death,
His will like torrents, not to be resisted,
Yet Law and Justice go along to guide him;
And what Law, or what Justice can he find
To justifie his Will? what Act or Statute,
By Humane, or Divine establishment,
Left to direct us, that makes Marriage death?
Honest fair Wedlock? 'twas given for encrease,
For preservation of Mankind I take it;
He must be more than man then that dare break it.
Come, dress ye handsomely, you shall have my jewels,
And put a face on that contemns base fortune,
'Twill make him more insult to see you fearful,
Outlook his anger.

EVANTHE
O my Valerio!
Be witness my pure mind, 'tis thee I grieve for.

QUEEN

But shew it not, I would so crucifie him
With an innocent neglect of what he can do,
A brave strong pious scorn, that I would shake him;
Put all the wanton Cupids in thine eyes,
And all the graces on that nature gave thee,
Make up thy beauty to that height of excellence,
I'll help thee, and forgive thee, as if Venus
Were now again to catch the god of War,
In his most rugged anger, when thou hast him,
(As 'tis impossible he should resist thee)
And kneeling at thy conquering feet for mercy,
Then shew thy Vertue, then again despise him,
And all his power, then with a look of honour
Mingled with noble chastity, strike him dead.

EVANTHE
Good Madam dress me,
You arm me bravely.

QUEEN
Make him know his cruelty
Begins with him first, he must suffer for it,
And that thy sentence is so welcome to thee,
And to thy noble Lord, you long to meet it.
Stamp such a deep impression of thy Beauty
Into his soul, and of thy worthiness,
That when Valerio and Evanthe sleep
In one rich earth, hung round about with blessings,
He may run mad, and curse his act; be lusty,
I'll teach thee how to dye too, if thou fear'st it.

EVANTHE
I thank your Grace, you have prepar'd me strongly,
And my weak mind.

QUEEN
Death is unwelcome never,
Unless it be to tortur'd minds and sick souls,
That make their own Hells; 'tis such a benefit
When it comes crown'd with honour, shews so sweet too!
Though they paint it ugly, that's but to restrain us,
For every living thing would love it else,
Fly boldly to their peace ere Nature call'd 'em;
The Rest we have from labour, and from trouble
Is some Incitement, every thing alike,
The poor Slave that lies private has his liberty,
As amply as his Master, in that Tomb
The Earth as light upon him, and the flowers

That grow about him, smell as sweet, and flourish.
But when we love with honour to our ends,
When Memory and Vertue are our Mourners;
What pleasure's there! they are infinite, Evanthe;
Only, my vertuous Wench, we want our senses,
That benefit we are barr'd, 'twould make us proud else,
And lazy to look up to happier life,
The Blessings of the people would so swell us.

EVANTHE
Good Madam, dress me, you have drest my soul,
The merriest Bride I'll be for all this misery,
The proudest to some Eyes too.

QUEEN
'Twill do better, come, shrink no more.

EVANTHE
I am too confident.

[Exeunt.

[Enter **FREDERICK** and **SORANO**.

SORANO
You are too remiss and wanton in your angers,
You mold things handsomely; and then neglect 'em;
A powerful Prince should be constant to his power still,
And hold up what he builds, then People fear him:
When he lets loose his hand it shews a weakness,
And men examine or contemn his greatness:
A scorn of this high kind should have call'd up
A revenge equal, not a pity in you.

FREDERICK
She is thy Sister.

SORANO
And she were my Mother,
Whilst I conceive 'tis you she has wrong'd, I hate her,
And shake her nearness off; I study, Sir,
To satisfie your angers that are just,
Before your pleasures.

FREDERICK
I have done that already,
I fear has pull'd too many curses on me.

SORANO
Curses or envies, on Valerio's head,
Would you take my counsel, Sir, they should all light,
And with the weight not only crack his scull,
But his fair credit; the exquisite vexation
I have devis'd, so please you give way in't,
And let it work, shall more afflict his soul,
And trench upon that honour that he brags of,
Than fear of Death in all the frights he carries;
If you sit down here they will both abuse ye,
Laugh at your poor relenting power, and scorn ye.
What satisfaction can their deaths bring to you,
That are prepar'd, and proud to dye, and willingly,
And at their ends will thank you for that honour?
How are you nearer the desire you aim at?
Or if it be revenge your anger covets,
How can their single deaths give you content, Sir?
Petty revenges end in blood, sleight angers,
A Princes rage should find out new diseases,
Death were a pleasure too, to pay proud fools with.

FREDERICK
What should I do?

SORANO
Add but your power unto me,
Make me but strong by your protection,
And you shall see what joy, and what delight,
What infinite pleasure this poor Month shall yield him.
I'll make him wish he were dead on his Marriage-day,
Or bed-rid with old age, I'll make him curse,
And cry and curse, give me but power.

FREDERICK
You have it,
Here, take my Ring, I am content he pay for't.

SORANO
It shall be now revenge, as I will handle it,
He shall live after this to beg his life too,
Twenty to one by this thread, as I'll weave it,
Evanthe shall be yours.

FREDERICK
Take all authority, and be most happy.

SORANO
Good Sir, no more pity.

[Exeunt.

[Enter **TONY**, three **CITIZENS** and three **WIVES**.

1ˢᵀ WIFE
Good Master Tony, put me in.

TONY
Where do you dwell?

1ˢᵀ WIFE
Forsooth, at the sign of the great Shoulder of Mutton.

TONY
A hungry man would hunt your house out instantly,
Keep the Dogs from your door; Is this Lettice Ruff your
Husband? a fine sharp sallet to your sign.

2ᴺᴰ WIFE
Will you put me in too?

3ᴿᴰ WIFE
And me, good Master Tony.

TONY
Put ye all in? you had best come twenty more; you
Think 'tis easie, a trick of legerdemain, to put ye all in,
'Twould pose a fellow that had twice my body,
Though it were all made into chines and fillets.

2ᴺᴰ WIFE
Put's into th' wedding, Sir, we would fain see that.

1ˢᵀ WIFE
And the brave Masque too.

TONY
You two are pretty women, are you their husbands?

2ᴺᴰ CITIZEN
Yes, for want of better.

TONY
I think so too, you would not be so mad else
To turn 'em loose to a company of young Courtiers,
That swarm like Bees in May, when they see young wenches;
You must not squeak.

3RD WIFE
No Sir, we are better tutor'd.

TONY
Nor if a young Lord offer you the courtesie—

2ND WIFE
We know what 'tis, Sir.

TONY
Nor you must not grumble,
If you be thrust up hard, we thrust most furiously.

1ST WIFE
We know the worst.

TONY
Get you two in then quietly,
And shift for your selves; we must have no old women,
They are out of use, unless they have petitions,
Besides they cough so loud they drown the Musick.
You would go in too, but there is no place for ye?
I am sorry for't, go and forget your wives,
Or pray they may be able to suffer patiently.
You may have Heirs may prove wise Aldermen,
Go, or I'le call the Guard.

3RD CITIZEN
We will get in, we'l venture broken pates else.

[Exit **CITIZENS** and **WOMEN**.

TONY
'Tis impossible,
You are too securely arm'd; how they flock hither,
And with what joy the women run by heaps
To see this Marriage! they tickle to think of it,
They hope for every month a husband too;
Still how they run, and how the wittals follow 'em,
The weak things that are worn between the leggs,
That brushing, dressing, nor new naps can mend,
How they post to see their own confusion!
This is a merry world.

[Enter **FREDERICK**.

FREDERICK

Look to the door Sirrah,
Thou art a fool, and may'st do mischief lawfully.

TONY
Give me your hand, you are my Brother fool,
You may both make the Law, and marr it presently.
Do you love a wench?

FREDERICK
Who does not, fool?

TONY
Not I, unless you will give me a longer lease to marry her.

FREDERICK
What are all these that come, what business have they?

TONY
Some come to gape, those are my fellow fools;
Some to get home their wives, those be their own fools;
Some to rejoyce with thee, those be the times fools;
And some I fear to curse thee, those are poor fools,

[Enter **CASSANDRA**, an old Lady passing over.

A set people call them honest. Look, look King, look,
A weather-beaten Lady new caresn'd.

FREDERICK
An old one.

TONY
The glasses of her eyes are new rub'd over,
And the worm-eaten records in her face are daub'd up neatly?
She layes her breasts out too, like to poch'd eggs
That had the yelks suckt out; they get new heads also,
New teeth, new tongues, for the old are all worn out,
And as 'tis hop'd, new tayls.

FREDERICK
For what?

TONY
For old Courtiers,
The young ones are too stirring for their travels.

FREDERICK
Go leave your knavery, and help to keep the door well,

I will have no such press.

TONY
Lay thy hand o'thy heart King.

FREDERICK
I'le have ye whipt.

TONY
The fool and thou art parted.

[Exit.

FREDERICK
Sorano work, and free me from this spell,
'Twixt love and scorn there's nothing felt but hell.

[Exit.

[Enter **VALERIO**, **CAMILLO**, **CLEANTHES**, **MENALLO** and **SERVANTS**.

VALERIO
Tye on my Scarf, you are so long about me,
Good my Lords help, give me my other Cloak,
That Hat and Feather, Lord what a Taylor's this,
To make me up thus straight! one sigh would burst me,
I have not room to breath, come button, button,
Button, apace.

CAMILLO
I am glad to see you merry Sir.

VALERIO
'Twould make you merry had you such a wife,
And such an age to injoy her in.

MENALLO
An age Sir?

VALERIO
A moneth's an age to him that is contented,
What should I seek for more? give me my sword.
Ha my good Lords, that every one of you now
Had but a Lady of that youth and beauty
To bless your selves this night with, would ye not?
Pray ye speak uprightly.

CLEANTHES

We confess ye happy,
And we could well wish such another Banquet,
But on that price my Lord—

VALERIO
'Twere nothing else,
No man can ever come to aim at Heaven,
But by the knowledge of a Hell. These shooes are heavy,
And if I should be call'd to dance they'l clog me,
Get me some pumps; I'le tell ye brave Camillo,
And you dear friends, the King has honour'd me,
Out of his gracious favour has much honour'd me,
To limit me my time, for who would live long?
Who would be old? 'tis such a weariness,
Such a disease, that hangs like lead upon us.
As it increases, so vexations,
Griefs of the minde, pains of the feeble body,
Rheums, coughs, catarrhs, we are but our living coffins;
Besides, the fair soul's old too, it grows covetous,
Which shews all honour is departed from us,
And we are Earth again.

CLEANTHES
You make fair use Sir.

VALERIO
I would not live to learn to lye Cleanthes
For all the world, old men are prone to that too;
Thou that hast been a Souldier, Menallo,
A noble Souldier, and defied all danger,
Adopted thy brave arm the heir to victory,
Would'st thou live so long till thy strength forsook thee?
Till thou grew'st only a long tedious story
Of what thou hadst been? till thy sword hang by,
And lazie Spiders fill'd the hilt with cobwebs?

MENALLO
No sure, I would not.

VALERIO
'Tis not fit ye should,
To dye a young man is to be an Angel,
Our great good parts put wings unto our souls:
We'l have a rouse before we go to bed friends,
Pray ye tell me, is't a hansome Mask we have?

CAMILLO
We understand so.

VALERIO
And the young gent. dance?

CLEANTHES
They do Sir, and some dance well.

VALERIO
They must before the Ladies,
We'l have a rouse before we go to bed friends,
A lusty one, 'twill make my blood dance too.

[Musick.

CAMILLO
Ten if you please.

VALERIO
And we'l be wondrous merry,
They stay sure, come, I hear the Musick forward,
You shall have all Gloves presently.

[Exit.

MENALLO
We attend Sir, but first we must look to th'
Doors.

[Knocking within.

The King has charged us.

[Exeunt.

[Enter two **SERVANTS**.

1ST SERVANT
What a noise do you keep there? call my fellows
O' the Guard; you must cease now untill the King be
Enter'd, he is gone to th' Temple now.

2ND SERVANT
Look to that back door, and keep it fast,
They swarm like Bees about it.

[Enter **CAMILLO, CLEANTHES, MENALLO, TONY** following.

CAMILLO

Keep back those Citizens, and let their wives in,
Their handsome wives.

TONY
They have crowded me to Verjuyce,
I sweat like a Butter-box.

1ST SERVANT
Stand further off there.

MENALLO
Take the women aside, and talk with 'em in private,
Give 'em that they came for.

TONY
The whole Court cannot do it;
Besides, the next Mask if we use 'em so,
They'l come by millions to expect our largess;
We have broke a hundred heads.

CLEANTHES
Are they so tender?

TONY
But 'twas behind, before they have all murrions.

CAMILLO
Let in those Ladies, make 'em room for shame there.

TONY
They are no Ladies, there's one bald before 'em,
A gent. bald, they are curtail'd queans in hired clothes,
They come out of Spain I think, they are very sultry.

MENALLO
Keep 'em in breath for an Embassadour.

[Knocks within.

Me thinks my nose shakes at their memories,
What bounsing's that?

WITHIN
I am one of the Musick Sir.

ANOTHER WITHIN
I have sweat-meats for the banquet.

CAMILLO
Let 'em in.

TONY
They lye my Lord, they come to seek their wives,
Two broken Citizens.

CAMILLO
Break 'em more, they are but brusled yet.
Bold Rascals, offer to disturb your wives?

CLEANTHES
Lock the doors fast, the Musick, hark, the King comes.

[A Curtain drawn.

[The **KING, QUEEN, VALERIO, EVANTHE, LADIES, ATTENDANTS, CAMILLO, CLEANTHES, SORANO, MENALLO.**

[A Mask.

[**CUPID** descends, the **GRACES** sitting by him, **CUPID** being bound the **GRACES** unbind him, he speaks.

CUPID
Unbind me, my delight, this night is mine,
Now let me look upon what Stars here shine,
Let me behold the beauties, then clap high
My cullor'd wings, proud of my Deity;
I am satisfied, bind me again, and fast,
My angry Bow will make too great a wast
Of beauty else, now call my Maskers in,
Call with a Song, and let the sports begin;
Call all my servants the effects of love,
And to a measure let them nobly move.
Come you servants of proud love,
Come away:
Fairly, nobly, gently move.
Too long, too long you make us stay;
Fancy, Desire, Delight, Hope, Fear,
Distrust and Jealousie, be you too here;
Consuming Care, and raging Ire,
And Poverty in poor attire,
March fairly in, and last Despair;
Now full Musick strike the Air.

[Enter the Maskers; **FANCY, DESIRE, DELIGHT, HOPE, FEAR, DISTRUST, JEALOUSIE, CARE, IRE, DESPAIR,** they dance, after which **CUPID** speaks.

CUPID
Away, I have done, the day begins to light,
Lovers, you know your fate, good night, good night.

[**CUPID** and the **GRACES** ascend in the Chariot.

KING
Come to the Banquet, when that's ended Sir,
I'le see you i' bed, and so good night; be merry,
You have a sweet bed-fellow.

VALERIO
I thank your Grace,
And ever shall be bound unto your nobleness.

KING
I pray I may deserve your thanks, set forward.

[Exeunt.

ACTUS TERTIUS

SCÆNA PRIMA

Enter divers **MONKS**, **ALPHONSO** going to the Tomb, **RUGIO**, and Friar **MARCO**, discover the Tomb and a Chair.

MARCO
The night grows on, lead softly to the Tomb,
And sing not till I bid ye; let the Musick
Play gently as he passes.

RUGIO
O fair picture,
That wert the living hope of all our honours;
How are we banisht from the joy we dreamt of!
Will he ne're speak more?

MARCO
'Tis full three moneths Lord Rugio,
Since any articulate sound came from his tongue,
Set him down gently.

[Sits in a Chair.

RUGIO

What should the reason be Sir?

MARCO
As 'tis in nature with those loving Husbands,
That sympathize their wives pains, and their throes
When they are breeding, and 'tis usuall too,
We have it by experience; so in him Sir,
In this most noble spirit that now suffers;
For when his honour'd Father good Brandino
Fell sick, he felt the griefs, and labour'd with them,
His fits and his disease he still inherited,
Grew the same thing, and had not nature check'd him,
Strength, and ability, he had dyed that hour too.

RUGIO
Embleme of noble love!

MARCO
That very minute
His Fathers breath forsook him, that same instant,
A rare example of his piety,
And love paternal, the Organ of his tongue
Was never heard to sound again; so near death
He seeks to wait upon his worthy Father,
But that we force his meat, he were one body.

RUGIO
He points to'th' Tomb.

MARCO
That is the place he honours,
A house I fear he will not be long out of.
He will to th' Tomb, good my Lord lend your hand;
Now sing the Funeral Song, and let him kneel,
For then he is pleas'd.

[A Song.

RUGIO
Heaven lend thy powerfull hand,
And ease this Prince.

MARCO
He will pass back again.

[Exeunt.

[Enter **VALERIO**.

VALERIO
They drink abundantly, I am hot with wine too,
Lustily warm, I'le steal now to my happiness,
'Tis midnight, and the silent hour invites me,
But she is up still, and attends the Queen;
Thou dew of wine and sleep hang on their eye-lids,
Steep their dull senses in the healths they drink,
That I may quickly find my lov'd Evanthe.
The King is merry too, and drank unto me,
Sign of fair peace, O this nights blessedness!
If I had forty heads I would give all for 't.
Is not the end of our ambitions,
Of all our humane studies, and our travels,
Of our desires, the obtaining of our wishes?
Certain it is, and there man makes his Center.
I have obtain'd Evanthe, I have married her,
Can any fortune keep me from injoying her?

[Enter **SORANO**.

I have my wish, what's left me to accuse now?
I am friends with all the world, but thy base malice;
Go glory in thy mischiefs thou proud man,
And cry it to the world thou hast ruin'd vertue;
How I contemn thee and thy petty malice!
And with what scorn, I look down on thy practice!

SORANO
You'l sing me a new Song anon Valerio,
And wish these hot words—

VALERIO
I despise thee fellow,
Thy threats, or flatteries, all I fling behind me;
I have my end, I have thy noble Sister,
A name too worthy of thy blood; I have married her,
And will injoy her too.

SORANO
'Tis very likely.

VALERIO
And that short moneth I have to bless me with her
I'le make an age, I'le reckon each embrace
A year of pleasure, and each night a Jubile,
Every quick kiss a Spring; and when I mean
To lose my self in all delightfulness,

Twenty sweet Summers I will tye together
In spight of thee, and thy malignant Master:
I will dye old in love, though young in pleasure.

SORANO
But that I hate thee deadly, I could pity thee,
Thou art the poorest miserable thing
This day on earth; I'le tell thee why Valerio,
All thou esteemest, and build'st upon for happiness,
For joy, for pleasure, for delight is past thee,
And like a wanton dream already vanisht.

VALERIO
Is my love false?

SORANO
No, she is constant to thee,
Constant to all thy misery she shall be,
And curse thee too.

VALERIO
Is my strong body weakn'd,
Charm'd, or abus'd with subtle drink? speak villain.

SORANO
Neither, I dare speak, thou art still as lusty
As when thou lov'dst her first, as strong and hopefull,
The month thou hast given thee is a month of misery,
And where thou think'st each hour shall yield a pleasure,
Look for a killing pain, for thou shalt find it
Before thou dyest, each minute shall prepare it,
And ring so many knels to sad afflictions;
The King has given thee a long month to dye in,
And miserably dye.

VALERIO
Undo thy Riddle,
I am prepar'd what ever fate shall follow.

SORANO
Dost thou see this Ring?

VALERIO
I know it too.

SORANO
Then mark me,
By vertue of this Ring this I pronounce to thee,

'Tis the Kings will.

VALERIO
Let me know it suddenly.

SORANO
If thou dost offer to touch Evanthes body
Beyond a kiss, though thou art married to her,
And lawfully as thou think'st may'st injoy her,
That minute she shall dye.

VALERIO
O Devil—

SORANO
If thou discover this command unto her,
Or to a friend that shall importune thee,
And why thou abstainest, and from whose will, ye all perish,
Upon the self-same forfeit: are ye fitted Sir?
Now if ye love her, ye may preserve her life still,
If not, you know the worst, how falls your month out?

VALERIO
This tyranny could never be invented
But in the school of Hell, Earth is too innocent;
Not to injoy her when she is my wife?
When she is willing too?

SORANO
She is most willing,
And will run mad to miss; but if you hit her,
Be sure you hit her home, and kill her with it;
There are such women that will dye with pleasure:
The Axe will follow else, that will not fail
To fetch her Maiden head, and dispatch her quickly;
Then shall the world know you are the cause of Murther,
And as 'tis requisite your life shall pay for't.

VALERIO
Thou dost but jest, thou canst not be so monstrous
As thou proclaim'st thy self; thou art her Brother,
And there must be a feeling heart within thee
Of her afflictions; wert thou a stranger to us,
And bred amongst wild rocks, thy nature wild too,
Affection in thee as thy breeding, cold,
And unrelenting as the rocks that nourisht thee,
Yet thou must shake to tell me this; they tremble
When the rude sea threatens divorce amongst 'em,

They that are senceless things shake at a tempest;
Thou art a man—

SORANO
Be thou too then, 'twill try thee,
And patience now will best become thy nobleness.

VALERIO
Invent some other torment to afflict me,
All, if thou please, put all afflictions on me,
Study thy brains out for 'em, so this be none
I care not of what nature, nor what cruelty,
Nor of what length.

SORANO
This is enough to vex ye.

VALERIO
The tale of Tantalus is now prov'd true,
And from me shall be registred Authentick;
To have my joyes within my arms, and lawfull,
Mine own delights, yet dare not touch.
Even as thou hatest me Brother, let no young man know this,
As thou shalt hope for peace when thou most needest it,
Peace in thy soul, desire the King to kill me,
Make me a traitor, any thing, I'le yield to it,
And give thee cause so I may dye immediately;
Lock me in Prison where no Sun may see me,
In walls so thick no hope may e're come at me;
Keep me from meat, and drink, and sleep, I'le bless thee;
Give me some damned potion to deliver me,
That I may never know my self again, forget
My Country, kindred, name and fortune; last,
That my chaste love may never appear before me,
This were some comfort.

SORANO
All I have I have brought ye,
And much good may it do ye my dear Brother,
See ye observe it well; you will find about ye
Many eyes set, that shall o're-look your actions,
If you transgress ye know, and so I leave ye.

[Exit.

VALERIO
Heaven be not angry, and I have some hope yet.

[Exit.

[Enter **FREDERICK** and **SORANO**.

FREDERICK
Hast thou been with him?

SORANO
Yes, and given him that Sir
Will make him curse his Birth; I told ye which way.
Did you but see him Sir, but look upon him,
With what a troubled and dejected nature
He walks now in a mist, with what a silence,
As if he were the shrowd he wrapt himself in,
And no more of Valerio but his shadow,
He seeks obscurity to hide his thoughts in,
You would wonder and admire for all you know it,
His jollity is down, valed to the ground Sir,
And his high hopes of full delights and pleasures
Are turn'd tormenters to him, strong diseases.

FREDERICK
But is there hope of her?

SORANO
It must fall necessary,
She must dislike him, quarrel with his person,
For women once deluded are next Devils,
And in the height of that opinion Sir,
You shall put on again, and she must meet ye.

FREDERICK
I am glad of this.

SORANO
I'le tell ye all the circumstance
Within this hour, but sure I heard your grace
To day as I attended, make some stops,
Some broken speeches, and some sighs between,
And then your Brothers name I heard distinctly,
And some sad wishes after.

FREDERICK
Ye are i'th' right Sir,
I would he were as sad as I could wish him,
Sad as the Earth.

SORANO

Would ye have it so?

FREDERICK
Thou hearest me,
Though he be sick with small hope of recovery,
That hope still lives, and mens eyes live upon it,
And in their eye their wishes; my Sorano,
Were he but cold once in the tomb he dotes on,
As 'tis the fittest place for melancholy,
My Court should be another Paradise,
And flow with all delights.

SORANO
Go to your pleasures, let me alone with this,
Hope shall not trouble ye, nor he three dayes.

FREDERICK
I shall be bound unto thee.

[Enter **VALERIO, CAMILLO, CLEANTHES, MENALLO.**

SORANO
I'le do it neatly too, no doubt shall catch me.

FREDERICK
Be gone, they are going to bed, I'le bid good night to 'em.

SORANO
And mark the man, you'l scarce know 'tis Valerio.

[Exit.

CAMILLO
Chear up my noble Lord, the minute's come,
You shall injoy the abstract of all sweetness,
We did you wrong, you need no wine to warm ye,
Desire shoots through your eyes like sudden wild-fires.

VALERIO
Beshrew me Lords, the wine has made me dull,
I am I know not what.

FREDERICK
Good pleasure to ye,
Good night and long too, as you find your appetite
You may fall to.

VALERIO

I do beseech your grace,
For which of all my loves and services
Have I deserved this?

FREDERICK
I am not bound to answer ye.

VALERIO
Nor I bound to obey in unjust actions.

FREDERICK
Do as you please, you know the penalty,
And as I have a soul it shall be executed;
Nay look not pale, I am not used to fear Sir,
If you respect your Lady, good night to ye.

[Exit.

VALERIO
But for respect to her and to my duty,
That reverent duty that I owe my Soveraign,
Which anger has no power to snatch me from,
The good night should be thine; good night for ever.
The King is wanton Lords, he would needs know of me
How many nick chases I would make to night.

MENALLO
My Lord, no doubt you'l prove a perfect gamester.

VALERIO
Faith no, I am unacquainted with the pleasure,
Bungle a set I may: how my heart trembles,
And beats my breast as it would break his way out!
Good night my noble friends.

CLEANTHES
Nay we must see you toward your bed my Lord.

VALERIO
Good faith it needs not,
'Tis late, and I shall trouble you.

CAMILLO
No, no, till the Bride come Sir.

VALERIO
I beseech you leave me,
You will make me bashfull else, I am so foolish,

Besides, I have some few devotions Lords,
And he that can pray with such a book in's arms—

CAMILLO
We'l leave ye then, and a sweet night wait upon ye.

MENALLO
And a sweet issue of this sweet night crown ye.

CLEANTHES
All nights and days be such till you grow old Sir.

[Exeunt **LORDS**.

VALERIO
I thank ye, 'tis a curse sufficient for me,
A labour'd one too, though you mean a blessing.
What shall I do? I am like a wretched Debtor,
That has a summe to tender on the forfeit
Of all he is worth, yet dare not offer it.
Other men see the Sun, yet I must wink at it;
And though I know 'tis perfect day, deny it:
My veins are all on fire, and burn like Ætna,
Youth and desire beat larums to my blood,
And adde fresh fuel to my warm affections.
I must injoy her, yet when I consider,
When I collect my self, and weigh her danger,
The tyrants will, and his power taught to murther,
My tender care controlls my blood within me,
And like a cold fit of a peevish Ague
Creeps to my soul, and flings an Ice upon me,

[Enter **QUEEN**, **EVANTHE**, **LADIES** and **FOOL**.

That locks all powers of youth up: but prevention—
O what a blessedness 'twere to be old now,
To be unable, bed-rid with diseases,
Or halt on Crutches to meet holy Hymen;
What a rare benefit! but I am curst,
That that speaks other men most freely happy,
And makes all eyes hang on their expectations,
Must prove the bane of me, youth, and ability.
She comes to bed, how shall I entertain her?

TONY
Nay I come after too, take the fool with ye,
For lightly he is ever one at Weddings.

QUEEN
Evanthe, make ye unready, your Lord staies for ye,
And prethee be merry.

TONY
Be very merry, Chicken,
Thy Lord will pipe to thee anon, and make thee dance too.

LADY
Will he so, good-man ass?

TONY
Yes good filly,
And you had such a Pipe, that piped so sweetly,
You would dance to death, you have learnt your sinque a pace.

EVANTHE
Your grace desires that that is too free in me,
I am merry at the heart.

TONY
Thou wilt be anon, the young smug boy will give thee a sweet cordial.

EVANTHE
I am so taken up in all my thoughts,
So possest Madam with the lawfull sweets
I shall this night partake of with my Lord,
So far transported (pardon my immodesty.)

VALERIO
Alas poor wench, how shall I recompence thee?

EVANTHE
That though they must be short, and snatcht away too,
E're they grow ripe, yet I shall far prefer 'em
Before a tedious pleasure with repentance.

VALERIO
O how my heart akes!

EVANTHE
Take off my Jewels Ladies,
And let my Ruff loose, I shall bid good night to ye,
My Lord staies here.

QUEEN
My wench, I thank thee heartily,
For learning how to use thy few hours handsomly,

They will be years I hope; off with your Gown now,
Lay down the bed there!

TONY
Shall I get into it and warm it for thee? a fools fire
is a fine thing,
And I'le so buss thee.

QUEEN
I'le have ye whipt ye Rascal.

TONY
That will provoke me more, I'le talk with thy husband,
He's a wise man I hope.

EVANTHE
Good night dear Madam,
Ladies, no further service, I am well,
I do beseech your grace to give us this leave,
My Lord and I to one another freely,
And privately, may do all other Ceremonies,
Women and Page we'l be to one another,
And trouble you no farther.

TONY
Art thou a wise man?

VALERIO
I cannot tell thee Tony, ask my neighbours.

TONY
If thou beest so, go lye with me to night,
The old fool will lye quieter than the young one,
And give thee more sleep, thou wilt look to morrow else
Worse than the prodigal fool the Ballad speaks of,
That was squeez'd through a horn.

VALERIO
I shall take thy counsel.

QUEEN
Why then good night, good night my best Evanthe,
My worthy maid, and as that name shall vanish,
A worthy wife, a long and happy; follow Sirrah.

EVANTHE
That shall be my care,
Goodness rest with your Grace.

QUEEN
Be lusty Lord, and take your Lady to ye,
And that power that shall part ye be unhappy.

VALERIO
Sweet rest unto ye, to ye all sweet Ladies;
Tony good night.

TONY
Shall not the fool stay with thee?

QUEEN
Come away Sirrah.

[Exeunt **QUEEN, LADIES.**

TONY
How the fool is sought for! sweet Malt is made of easie fire,
A hasty horse will quickly tire, a sudden leaper sticks i'th' mire,
Phlebotomy and the word lye nigher, take heed of friend I thee require;
This from an Almanack I stole, and learnt this Lesson from a fool.
Good night my Bird.

[Exit **TONY.**

EVANTHE
Good night wise Master Tony;
Will ye to bed my Lord? Come, let me help ye.

VALERIO
To bed Evanthe, art thou sleepy?

EVANTHE
No, I shall be worse if you look sad upon me,
Pray ye let's to bed.

VALERIO
I am not well my love.

EVANTHE
I'le make ye well, there's no such Physick for ye
As your warm Mistris arms.

VALERIO
Art thou so cunning?

EVANTHE

I speak not by experience, 'pray ye mistake not;
But if you love me—

VALERIO
I do love so dearly,
So much above the base bent of desire,
I know not how to answer thee.

EVANTHE
To bed then,
There I shall better credit ye; fie my Lord,
Will ye put a maid to't, to teach ye what to do?
An innocent maid? Are ye so cold a Lover?
In truth you make me blush, 'tis midnight too,
And 'tis no stoln love, but authorised openly,
No sin we covet, pray let me undress ye,
You shall help me; prethee sweet Valerio;
Be not so sad, the King will be more mercifull.

VALERIO
May not I love thy mind?

EVANTHE
And I yours too,
'Tis a most noble one, adorn'd with vertue;
But if we love not one another really,
And put our bodies and our mind together,
And so make up the concord of affection,
Our love will prove but a blind superstition:
This is no school to argue in my Lord,
Nor have we time to talk away allow'd us,
Pray let's dispatch, if any one should come
And find us at this distance, what would they think?
Come, kiss me and to bed.

VALERIO
That I dare do, and kiss again.

EVANTHE
Spare not, they are your own Sir.

VALERIO
But to injoy thee is to be luxurious;
Too sensuall in my love, and too ambitious;
O how I burn! to pluck thee from the stalk,
Where now thou grow'st a sweet bud and a beauteous,
And bear'st the prime and honour of the Garden,
Is but to violate thy spring, and spoil thee.

EVANTHE

To let me blow, and fall alone would anger ye.

VALERIO

Let's sit together thus, and as we sit
Feed on the sweets of one anothers souls,
The happiness of love is contemplation,
The blessedness of love is pure affection,
Where no allay of actuall dull desires,
Of pleasure that partakes with wantonness,
Of humane fire that burns out as it kindles,
And leaves the body but a poor repentance,
Can ever mix, let's fix on that Evanthe,
That's everlasting, the tother casuall;
Eternity breeds one, the other fortune,
Blind as her self, and full of all afflictions.
Shall we love vertuously?

EVANTHE

I ever loved so.

VALERIO

And only think our love; the rarest pleasure,
And that we most desire, let it be humane,
If once injoyed grows stale, and cloys our appetites;
I would not lessen in my love for any thing,
Nor find thee but the same in my short journey,
For my loves safety.

EVANTHE

Now I see I am old Sir,
Old and ill favour'd too, poor and despis'd,
And am not worth your noble Fellowship,
Your fellowship in Love, you would not else
Thus cunningly seek to betray a maid,
A maid that honours you thus piously;
Strive to abuse the pious love she brings ye.
Farewel my Lord, since ye have a better Mistris,
For it must seem so, or ye are no man,
A younger, happier, I shall give her room,
So much I love ye still.

VALERIO

Stay my Evanthe,
Heaven bear me witness, thou art all I love,
All I desire, and now have pity on me,
I never lyed before; forgive me Justice,

Youth and affection stop your ears unto me.

EVANTHE
Why do you weep? if I have spoke too harshly,
And unbeseeming, my beloved Lord,
My care and duty, pardon me.

VALERIO
O hear me,
Hear me Evanthe; I am all on torture,
And this lye tears my conscience as I vent it;
I am no man.

EVANTHE
How Sir?

VALERIO
No man for pleasure, no womans man.

EVANTHE
Goodness forbid my Lord, sure you abuse your self.

VALERIO
'Tis true Evanthe;
I shame to say you will find it.

[Weeps.

EVANTHE
He weeps bitterly,
'Tis my hard fortune, bless all young maids from it;
Is there no help my Lord in art will comfort ye?

VALERIO
I hope there is.

EVANTHE
How long have you been destitute?

VALERIO
Since I was young.

EVANTHE
'Tis hard to dye for nothing,
Now you shall know 'tis not the pleasure Sir,
(For I am compell'd to love you spiritually)
That women aim at, I affect ye for,
'Tis for your worth; and kiss me, be at peace,

Because I ever loved ye, I still honour ye,
And with all duty to my Husband follow ye;
Will ye to bed now? ye are asham'd it seems;
Pygmalion pray'd and his cold stone took life,
You do not know with what zeal I shall ask Sir,
And what rare miracle that may work upon ye;
Still blush? prescribe your Law.

VALERIO
I prethee pardon me,
To bed, and I'le sit by thee, and mourn with thee,
Mourn both our fortunes, our unhappy ones:
Do not despise me, make me not more wretched,
I pray to Heaven when I am gone Evanthe,
As my poor date is but a span of time now,
To recompence thy noble patience,
Thy love and vertue with a fruitfull husband,
Honest and honourable.

EVANTHE
Come, you have made me weep now,
All fond desire dye here, and welcom chastity,
Honour and chastity, do what you please Sir.

[Exeunt.

ACTUS QUARTUS

SCÆNA PRIMA

Enter at one door **RUGIO** and Frier **MARCO**, at the other door **SORANO**, with a little glass viol.

RUGIO
What ails this piece of mischief to look sad?
He seems to weep too.

MARCO
Something is a hatching,
And of some bloody nature too, Lord Rugio,
This Crocodile mourns thus cunningly.

SORANO
Hail holy Father,
And good day to the good Lord Rugio,
How fares the sad Prince I beseech ye Sir?

RUGIO

'Tis like you know, you need not ask that question,
You have your eyes and watches on his miseries
As near as ours, I would they were as tender.

MARCO

Can you do him good? as the King and you appointed him,
So he is still, as you desir'd I think too,
For every day he is worse (Heaven pardon all)
Put off your sorrow, you may laugh now Lord,
He cannot last long to disturb your Master,
You have done worthy service to his Brother,
And he most memorable love.

SORANO

You do not know Sir
With what remorse I ask, nor with what weariness
I groan and bow under this load of honour,
And how my soul sighs for the beastly services,
I have done his pleasures, these be witness with me,
And from your piety believe me Father,
I would as willingly unclothe my self
Of title, that becomes me not I know;
Good men, and great names best agree together;
Cast off the glorious favours, and the trappings
Of sound and honour, wealth and promises,
His wanton pleasures have flung on my weakness,
And chuse to serve my countries cause and vertues,
Poorly and honestly, and redeem my ruines,
As I would hope remission of my mischiefs.

RUGIO

Old and experienc'd men, my Lord Sorano,
Are not so quickly caught with gilt hypocrisie,
You pull your claws in now and fawn upon us,
As lyons do to intice poor foolish beasts;
And beasts we should be too if we believ'd ye,
Go exercise your Art.

SORANO

For Heaven sake scorn me not,
Nor adde more Hell to my afflicted soul
Than I feel here; as you are honourable,
As you are charitable look gently on me,
I will no more to Court, be no more Devil,
I know I must be hated even of him
That was my Love now, and the more he loves me
For his foul ends, when they shall once appear to him,

Muster before his conscience and accuse him,
The fouler and the more falls his displeasure,
Princes are fading things, so are their favours.

MARCO
He weeps again, his heart is toucht sure with remorse.

SORANO
See this, and give me fair attention good my Lord,
And worthy Father see, within this viol
The remedy and cure of all my honour,
And of the sad Prince lyes.

RUGIO
What new trick's this?

SORANO
'Tis true, I have done Offices abundantly
Ill and prodigious to the Prince Alphonso,
And whilst I was a knave I sought his death too.

RUGIO
You are too late convicted to be good yet.

SORANO
But Father, when I felt this part afflict me,
This inward part, and call'd me to an audit
Of my misdeeds and mischiefs—

MARCO
Well, go on Sir.

SORANO
O then, then, then what was my glory then Father?
The favour of the King, what did that ease me?
What was it to be bow'd to by all creatures?
Worshipt, and courted, what did this avail me?
I was a wretch, a poor lost wretch.

MARCO
Still better.

SORANO
Till in the midst of all my grief I found
Repentance, and a learned man to give the means to it,
A Jew, an honest and a rare Physician,
Of him I had this Jewel; 'tis a Jewel,
And at the price of all my wealth I bought it:

If the King knew it I must lose my head,
And willingly, most willingly I would suffer,
A child may take it, 'tis so sweet in working.

MARCO
To whom would you apply it?

SORANO
To the sick Prince,
It will in half a day dissolve his melancholy.

RUGIO
I do believe, and give him sleep for ever.
What impudence is this, and what base malice,
To make us instruments of thy abuses?
Are we set here to poison him?

SORANO
Mistake not, yet I must needs say, 'tis a noble care,
And worthy vertuous servants; if you will see
A flourishing estate again in Naples,
And great Alphonso reign that's truly good,
And like himself able to make all excellent;
Give him this drink, and this good health unto him.

[Drinks.

I am not so desperate yet to kill my self,
Never look on me as a guilty man,
Nor on the water as a speedy poison:
I am not mad, nor laid out all my treasure,
My conscience and my credit to abuse ye;
How nimbly and how chearfully it works now
Upon my heart and head! sure I am a new man,
There is no sadness that I feel within me,
But as it meets it, like a lazie vapour
How it flyes off. Here, give it him with speed,
You are more guilty than I ever was,
And worthier of the name of evil subjects,
If but an hour you hold this from his health.

RUGIO
'Tis some rare vertuous thing sure, he is a good man,
It must be so, come, let's apply it presently,
And may it sweetly work.

SORANO
Pray let me hear on't, and carry it close my Lords.

MARCO
Yes, good Sorano.

[Exit **RUGIO**, **MARCO**.

SORANO
Do my good fools, my honest pious coxcombs,
My wary fools too: have I caught your wisedoms?
You never dream't I knew an Antidote,
Nor how to take it to secure mine own life;
I am an Asse, go, give him the fine cordial,
And when you have done go dig his grave, good Frier,
Some two hours hence we shall have such a bawling,
And roaring up and down for Aqua vitæ,
Such rubbing, and such nointing, and such cooling,
I have sent him that will make a bonfire in's belly,
If he recover it, there is no heat in Hell sure.

[Exit.

[Enter **FREDERICK** and **PODRAMO**.

FREDERICK
Podramo?

PODRAMO
Sir.

FREDERICK
Call hither Lord Valerio, and let none trouble us.

PODRAMO
It shall be done Sir.

[Exit.

FREDERICK
I know he wants no additions to his tortures,
He has enough for humane blood to carry,
Yet I must vex him further;
So many that I wonder his hot youth
And high-bred spirit breaks not into fury;
I must yet torture him a little further,
And make my self sport with his miseries,
My anger is too poor else. Here he comes,

[Enter **VALERIO**.

Now my young married Lord, how do you feel your self?
You have the happiness you ever aim'd at,
The joy and pleasure.

VALERIO
Would you had the like Sir.

FREDERICK
You tumble in delights with your sweet Lady,
And draw the minutes out in dear embraces,
You live a right Lords life.

VALERIO
Would you had tryed it,
That you might know the vertue but to suffer,
Your anger though it be unjust and insolent,
Sits handsomer upon you than your scorn,
To do a wilfull ill and glory in it,
Is to do it double, double to be damn'd too.

FREDERICK
Hast thou not found a loving and free Prince,
High in his favours too; that has confer'd
Such hearts ease, and such heaps of comfort on thee,
All thou cou'dst ask?

VALERIO
You are grown a tyrant too
Upon so suffering, and so still a subject;
You have put upon me such a punishment,
That if your youth were honest it would blush at:
But you are a shame to nature, as to vertue.
Pull not my rage upon ye, 'tis so just,
It will give way to no respect; my life,
My innocent life, I dare maintain it Sir,
Like a wanton prodigal you have flung away,
Had I a thousand more I would allow 'em,
And be as careless of 'em as your will is;
But to deny those rights the Law hath given me,
The holy Law, and make her life the penance,
Is such a studied and unheard of malice,
No heart that is not hired from Hell dare think of;
To do it then too, when my hopes were high,
High as my Blood, all my desires upon me,
My free affections ready to embrace her,

[Enter **CASSANDRA**.

And she mine own; do you smile at this? is't done well?
Is there not Heaven above you that sees all?

[Exit **VALERIO**.

FREDERICK
Come hither Time, how does your noble Mistriss?

CASSANDRA
As a Gentlewoman may do in her case that's newly married, Sir:
Sickly sometimes, and fond on't, like your Majesty.

FREDERICK
She is breeding then?

CASSANDRA
She wants much of her colour,
And has her qualms as Ladies use to have, Sir,
And her disgusts.

FREDERICK
And keeps her Chamber?

CASSANDRA
Yes Sir.

FREDERICK
And eats good Broths and Jellies.

CASSANDRA
I am sure she sighs, Sir, and weeps, good Lady.

FREDERICK
Alas, good Lady, for it,
She should have one could comfort her, Cassandra,
Could turn those tears to joys, a lusty Comforter.

CASSANDRA
A comfortable man does well at all hours,
For he brings comfortable things.

FREDERICK
Come hither, & hold your fann between, you have eaten Onions,
Her breath stinks like a Fox, her teeth are contagious,
These old women are all Elder-Pipes, do ye mark me?

[Gives a Purse.

CASSANDRA
Yes, Sir, but does your Grace think I am fit,
That am both old and vertuous?

FREDERICK
Therefore the fitter, the older still the better,
I know thou art as holy as an old Cope,
Yet upon necessary use—

CASSANDRA
'Tis true, Sir.

FREDERICK
Her feeling sense is fierce still, speak unto her,
You are familiar; speak I say, unto her,
Speak to the purpose; tell her this, and this.

CASSANDRA
Alas, she is honest, Sir, she is very honest,
And would you have my gravity—

FREDERICK
I, I, your gravity will become the cause the better,
I'll look thee out a Knight shall make thee a Lady too,
A lusty Knight, and one that shall be ruled by thee,
And add to these, I'll make 'em good, no mincing,
Nor ducking out of nicety, good Lady,
But do it home, we'll all be friends too, tell her,
And such a joy—

CASSANDRA
That's it that stirs me up, Sir,
I would not for the World attempt her Chastity,
But that they may live lovingly hereafter.

FREDERICK
For that I urge it too.

CASSANDRA
A little evil may well be suffered for a general good, Sir,
I'll take my leave of your Majesty.

[Exit.

[Enter **VALERIO**.

FREDERICK

Go fortunately, be speedy too: here comes Valerio,
If his affliction have allayed his spirit
My work has end. Come hither, Lord Valerio,
How do you now?

VALERIO
Your Majesty may guess,
Not so well, nor so fortunate as you are,
That can tye up mens honest wills, and actions.

FREDERICK
You clearly see now, brave Valerio,
What 'tis to be the Rival to a Prince,
To interpose against a raging Lion;
I know you have suffer'd, infinitely suffer'd,
And with a kind of pity I behold it,
And if you dare be worthy of my mercy,
I can yet heal you; yield up your Evanthe,
Take off my sentence also.

VALERIO
I fall thus low, Sir,
My poor sad heart under your feet I lay,
And all the service of my life.

FREDERICK
Do this then, for without this 'twill be impossible,
Part with her for a while.

VALERIO
You have parted us,
What should I do with that I cannot use Sir?

FREDERICK
'Tis well consider'd, let me have the Lady,
And thou shalt see how nobly I'll befriend thee,
How all this difference—

VALERIO
Will she come do you think, Sir?

FREDERICK
She must be wrought, I know she is too modest,
And gently wrought, and cunningly.

VALERIO
'Tis fit, Sir.

FREDERICK
And secretly it must be done.

VALERIO
As thought.

FREDERICK
I'll warrant ye her honour shall be fair still,
No soil nor stain shall appear on that, Valerio,
You see a thousand that bear sober faces,
And shew of as inimitable modesties;
You would be sworn too that they were pure Matrons,
And most chaste maids: and yet to augment their fortunes,
And get them noble friends—

VALERIO
They are content, Sir,
In private to bestow their Beauties on 'em.

FREDERICK
They are so, and they are wise, they know no want for't,
Nor no eye sees they want their honesties.

VALERIO
If it might be carried thus.

FREDERICK
It shall be, Sir.

VALERIO
I'll see you dead first, with this caution,
Why, sure I think it might be done.

FREDERICK
Yes, easily.

VALERIO
For what time would your Grace desire her Body?

FREDERICK
A month or two, it shall be carried still
As if she kept with you, and were a stranger,
Rather a hater of the grace I offer;
And then I will return her with such honour—

VALERIO
'Tis very like I dote much on your Honour.

FREDERICK
And load her with such favour too, Valerio—

VALERIO
She never shall claw off? I humbly thank ye.

FREDERICK
I'll make ye both the happiest, and the richest,
And the mightiest too—

VALERIO
But who shall work her, Sir?
For on my Conscience she is very honest,
And will be hard to cut as a rough Diamond.

FREDERICK
Why, you must work her, any thing from your tongue,
Set off with golden, and perswasive Language,
Urging your dangers too.

VALERIO
But all this time
Have you the conscience, Sir, to leave me nothing,
Nothing to play withal?

FREDERICK
There be a thousand, take where thou wilt.

VALERIO
May I make bold with your Queen,
She is useless to your Grace, as it appears, Sir,
And but a loyal Wife that may be lost too;
I have a mind to her, and then 'tis equal?

FREDERICK
How, Sir?

VALERIO
'Tis so, Sir, thou most glorious impudence,
Have I not wrongs enow to suffer under,
But thou must pick me out to make a Monster?
A hated Wonder to the World? Do you start
At my intrenching on your private liberty,
And would you force a high-way through mine honour,
And make me pave it too? But that thy Queen
Is of that excellent honesty,
And guarded with Divinity about her,
No loose thought can come near, nor flame unhallowed,

I would so right my self.

FREDERICK
Why, take her to ye,
I am not vex'd at this, thou shalt enjoy her,
I'll be thy friend if that may win thy courtesie.

VALERIO
I will not be your Bawd, though for your Royalty.
Was I brought up, and nourish'd in the Court,
With thy most Royal Brother, and thy self,
Upon thy Fathers charge, thy happy Fathers,
And suckt the sweetness of all humane arts,
Learn'd Arms and Honour, to become a Rascal;
Was this the expectation of my Youth,
My growth of Honour? Do you speak this truly,
Or do you try me, Sir? for I believe not,
At least I would not, and methinks 'tis impossible
There should be such a Devil in a Kings shape,
Such a malignant Fiend.

FREDERICK
I thank ye, Sir,
To morrow is your last day, and look to it,
Get from my sight, away.

VALERIO
Ye are—Oh, my heart's too high and full to think upon ye.

[Exeunt.

[Enter **EVANTHE** and **CASSANDRA**.

EVANTHE
You think it fit then, mortified Cassandra,
That I should be a Whore?

CASSANDRA
Why a Whore, Madam?
If every Woman that upon necessity
Did a good turn, for there's the main point, mark it,
Were term'd a Whore, who would be honest, Madam?
Your Lords life, and your own are now in hazard,
Two precious lives may be redeem'd with nothing,
Little or nothing; say an hours or days sport,
Or such a toy, the end to it is wantonness.
(That we call lust that maidens lose their fame for)
But a compell'd necessity of honour,

Fair as the day, and clear as innocence,
Upon my life and conscience, a direct way—

EVANTHE
To be a Rascal.

CASSANDRA
'Tis a kind of Rape too,
That keeps you clear, for where your will's compell'd
Though you yield up your Body you are safe still.

EVANTHE
Thou art grown a learned Bawd, I ever look'd
Thy great sufficiency would break out.

CASSANDRA
You may,
You that are young, and fair scorn us old Creatures,
But you must know my years, ere you be wise, Lady,
And my experience too; say the King loved ye?
Say it were nothing else?

EVANTHE
I, marry wench, now thou comest to me.

CASSANDRA
Do you think Princes favours are such sleight things,
To fling away when you please? there be young Ladies
Both fair and honourable, that would leap to reach 'em,
And leap aloft too.

EVANTHE
Such are light enough;
I am no Vaulter, Wench, but canst thou tell me,
Though he be a King, whether he be sound or no?
I would not give my Youth up to infection.

CASSANDRA
As sound as honour ought to be, I think, Lady;
Go to, be wise, I do not bid you try him;
But if he love you well, and you neglect him,
Your Lords life hanging on the hazard of it,
If you be so wilful proud.

EVANTHE
Thou speakest to the point still;
But when I have lain with him, what am I then, Gentlewoman?

CASSANDRA
What are you? why, the same you are now, a woman,
A vertuous Woman, and a noble Woman,
Touching at what is noble, you become so.
Had Lucrece e'r been thought of but for Tarquin?
She was before a simple unknown Woman,
When she was ravish'd, she was a reverend Saint;
And do you think she yielded not a little?
And had a kind of will to have been re-ravish'd?
Believe it, yes: there are a thousand stories
Of wondrous loyal Women, that have slipt,
But it has been on the ice of tender honour,
That kept 'em cool still to the World. I think you are blest,
That have such an occasion in your hands to beget a Chronicle,
A faithful one.

EVANTHE
It must needs be much honour.

CASSANDRA
As you may make it, infinite, and safe too,
And when 'tis done, your Lord and you may live
So quietly, and peaceably together,
And be what you please.

EVANTHE
But suppose this, Wench,
The King should so delight me with his Company,
I should forget my Lord, and no more look on him.

CASSANDRA
That's the main hazard, for I tell you truly,
I have heard report speak he is an infinite pleasure,
Almost above belief; there be some Ladies,
And modest to the world too, wondrous modest,
That have had the blessedness to try his body,
That I have heard proclaim him a new Hercules.

EVANTHE
So strongly able?

CASSANDRA
There will be the danger,
You being but a young and tender Lady,
Although your mind be good, yet your weak Body,
At first encounter too, to meet with one
Of his unconquer'd strength.

EVANTHE

Peace, thou rude Bawd,
Thou studied old corruptness, tye thy tongue up,
Your hired base tongue; is this your timely counsel?
Dost thou seek to make me dote on wickedness?
Because 'tis ten times worse than thou deliver'st it?
To be a Whore, because he has sufficiency
To make a hundred? O thou impudence!
Have I reliev'd thy Age to mine own ruine?
And worn thee in my Bosome, to betray me?
Can years and impotence win nothing on thee
That's good and honest, but thou must go on still?
And where thy bloud wants heat to sin thy self,
Force thy decrepit will to make me wicked?

CASSANDRA

I did but tell ye.

EVANTHE

What the damnedst Woman,
The cunning'st and the skilfull'st Bawd comes short of;
If thou hadst liv'd ten Ages to be damn'd in,
And exercis'd this Art the Devil taught thee,
Thou could'st not have express'd it more exactly.

CASSANDRA

I did not bid you sin.

EVANTHE

Thou woo'd'st me to it,
Thou that art fit for Prayer and the Grave,
Thy Body Earth already, and Corruption,
Thou taught'st the way; go follow your fine function,
There are houses of delight, that want good Matrons,
Such grave Instructors, get thee thither, Monster,
And read variety of sins to wantons,
And when they roar with pains, learn to make plaisters.

CASSANDRA

This we have for our good wills.

EVANTHE

If e'r I see thee more,
Or any thing that's like thee, to affright me,
By this fair light I'll spoil thy Bawdery,
I'll leave thee neither Eyes nor Nose to grace thee.
When thou wantest Bread, and common pity towards thee,

[Enter **FREDERICK**.

And art a starving in a Ditch, think of me,
Then dye, and let the wandring Bawds lament thee;
Be gone, I charge thee leave me.

CASSANDRA
You'll repent this.

[Exit.

FREDERICK
She's angry, and t'other crying too, my suit's cold.
I'll make your heart ake, stubborn Wench, for this;
Turn not so angry from me, I will speak to you,
Are you grown proud with your delight, good Lady,
So pamper'd with your sport you scorn to know me?

EVANTHE
I scorn ye not, I would you scorn'd not me, Sir,
And forc't me to be weary of my duty,
I know your Grace, would I had never seen ye.

FREDERICK
Because I love you, because I dote upon ye,
Because I am a man that seek to please ye.

EVANTHE
I have man enough already to content me,
As much, as noble, and as worthy of me,
As all the World can yield.

FREDERICK
That's but your modesty,
You have no man, nay never look upon me,
I know it, Lady, no man to content ye,
No man that can, or at the least, that dares,
Which is a poorer man, and nearer nothing.

EVANTHE
Be nobler, Sir, inform'd.

FREDERICK
I'll tell thee, Wench,
The poor condition of this poorer fellow,
And make thee blush for shame at thine own errour,
He never tendred yet a husbands duty,
To thy warm longing bed.

EVANTHE

How should he know that?

FREDERICK

I am sure he did not, for I charg'd him no,
Upon his life I charg'd him, but to try him;
Could any brave or noble spirit stop here?
Was life to be preferr'd before affection?
Lawful and long'd for too?

EVANTHE

Did you command him?

FREDERICK

I did in policy to try his spirit.

EVANTHE

And could he be so dead cold to observe it?
Brought I no beauty, nor no love along with me?

FREDERICK

Why, that is it that makes me scorn to name him.
I should have lov'd him if he had ventur'd for't,
Nay, doted on his bravery.

EVANTHE

Only charg'd?
And with that spell sit down? dare men fight bravely
For poor slight things, for drink, or ostentation?
And there indanger both their lives and fortunes,
And for their lawful loves fly off with fear?

FREDERICK

'Tis true, and with a cunning base fear too to abuse thee?
Made thee believe, poor innocent Evanthe,
Wretched young Girl, it was his impotency;
Was it not so? deny it.

EVANTHE

O my anger! at my years to be cozen'd with a young man!

FREDERICK

A strong man too, certain he lov'd ye dearly.

EVANTHE

To have my shame and love mingled together,
And both flung on me like a weight to sink me,

I would have dyed a thousand times.

FREDERICK
So would any,
Any that had the spirit of a man;
I would have been kill'd in your arms.

EVANTHE
I would he had been,
And buried in mine arms, that had been noble,
And what a monument would I have made him?
Upon this breast he should have slept in peace,
Honour, and everlasting love his mourners;
And I still weeping till old time had turn'd me,
And pitying powers above into pure crystal.

FREDERICK
Hadst thou lov'd me, and had my way been stuck
With deaths, as thick as frosty nights with stars,
I would have ventur'd.

EVANTHE
Sure there is some trick in't: Valerio ne'r was Coward.

FREDERICK
Worse than this too,
Tamer, and seasoning of a baser nature,
He set your woman on ye to betray ye,
Your bawdy woman, or your sin solicitor;
I pray but think what this man may deserve now,
I know he did, and did it to please me too.

EVANTHE
Good Sir afflict me not too fast, I feel
I am a woman, and a wrong'd one too,
And sensible I am of my abuses,
Sir, you have loved me.

FREDERICK
And I love thee still, pity thy wrongs, and dote upon
thy person.

EVANTHE
To set my woman on me 'twas too base, Sir.

FREDERICK
Abominable vile.

EVANTHE

But I shall fit him.

FREDERICK

All reason and all Law allows it to ye,
And ye are a fool, a tame fool, if you spare him.

EVANTHE

You may speak now, and happily prevail too,
And I beseech your Grace be angry with me.

FREDERICK

I am at heart. She staggers in her faith,
And will fall off I hope, I'll ply her still.
Thou abused innocence, I suffer with thee,
If I should give him life, he would still betray thee;
That fool that fears to dye for such a Beauty,
Would for the same fear sell thee unto misery.
I do not say he would have been Bawd himself too.

EVANTHE

Follow'd thus far? nay then I smell the malice,
It tastes too hot of practis'd wickedness,
There can be no such man, I am sure no Gentleman;
Shall my anger make me whore, and not my pleasure?
My sudden inconsiderate rage abuse me?
Come home again, my frighted faith, my vertue,
Home to my heart again; he be a Bawd too?

FREDERICK

I will not say he offered fair Evanthe.

EVANTHE

Nor do not dare, 'twill be an impudence,
And not an honour for a Prince to lye;
Fye, Sir, a person of your rank to trifle,
I know you do lye.

FREDERICK

How?

EVANTHE

Lye shamefully, and I could wish myself a man but one day,
To tell you openly you lye too basely.

FREDERICK

Take heed, wild fool.

EVANTHE

Take thou heed, thou tame Devil,
Thou all Pandora's Box in a Kings figure,
Thou hast almost whor'd my weak belief already,
And like an Engineer blown up mine honour;
But I shall countermine, and catch your mischief,
This little Fort you seek, I shall man nobly,
And strongly too, with chaste obedience
To my dear Lord, with vertuous thoughts that scorn ye.
Victorious Thomyris ne'r won more honour
In cutting off the Royal head of Cyrus,
Than I shall do in conquering thee; farewel,
And if thou canst be wise, learn to be good too.
'Twill give thee nobler lights than both thine eyes do;
My poor Lord and my self are bound to suffer,
And when I see him faint under your sentence,
I'll tell ye more, it may be then I'll yield too.

FREDERICK

Fool unexampled, shall my anger follow thee?

[Exeunt.

[Enter **RUGIO** and Friar **MARCO**, amazed.

RUGIO

Curst on our sights, our fond credulities,
A thousand curses on the Slave that cheated us,
The damn'd Slave.

MARCO

We have e'n sham'd our service,
Brought our best care and loyalties to nothing,
'Tis the most fearful poyson, the most potent,
Heaven give him patience; Oh it works most strongly,
And tears him, Lord.

RUGIO

That we should be so stupid
To trust the arrant'st Villain that e'r flatter'd,
The bloodiest too, to believe a few soft words from him,
And give way to his prepar'd tears.

WITHIN

Alphonso. Oh, Oh, Oh.

RUGIO

Hark, Fryar Marco, hark, the poor Prince, that

we should be such Block-heads,
As to be taken with his drinking first!
And never think what Antidotes are made for!
Two wooden sculls we have, and we deserve to be hang'd for't;
For certainly it will be laid to our charge;
As certain too, it will dispatch him speedily,
Which way to turn, or what to—

MARCO
Let's pray, Heavens hand is strong.

RUGIO
The poyson's strong, you would say.

[Enter **ALPHONSO**, carried on a Couch by two **FRIARS**.

Would any thing—He comes, let's give him comfort.

ALPHONSO
Give me more air, air, more air, blow, blow,
Open thou Eastern Gate, and blow upon me,
Distill thy cold dews, O thou icy Moon,
And Rivers run through my afflicted spirit.
I am all fire, fire, fire, the raging dog star
Reigns in my bloud, Oh which way shall I turn me?
Ætna, and all his flames burn in my head,
Fling me into the Ocean or I perish;
Dig, dig, dig, till the Springs fly up,
The cold, cold Springs, that I may leap into 'em,
And bathe my scorcht Limbs in their purling Pleasures.
Or shoot me up into the higher Region,
Where treasures of delicious Snow are nourisht,
And Banquets of sweet Hail.

RUGIO
Hold him fast Fryer, O how he burns!

ALPHONSO
What will ye sacrifice me?
Upon the Altar lay my willing body,
And pile your Wood up, fling your holy incense;
And as I turn me you shall see all flame,
Consuming flame, stand off me, or you are ashes.

BOTH
Most miserable wretches.

ALPHONSO

Bring hither Charity
And let me hug her, Fryer, they say she's cold,
Infinite cold Devotion cannot warm her;
Draw me a river of false lovers tears
Clean through my breast, they are dull, cold, and forgetful,
And will give ease, let Virgins sigh upon me,
Forsaken souls, the sighs are precious,
Let them all sigh: Oh hell, hell, hell, Oh horror.

MARCO
To bed, good Sir.

ALPHONSO
My bed will burn about me,
Like Phaeton, in all consuming flashes
I am inclosed, let me fly, let me fly, give room;
Betwixt the cold Bear, and the raging Lyon
Lyes my safe way; O for a cake of Ice now,
To clap unto my heart to comfort me;
Decrepit Winter hang upon my shoulders,
And let me wear thy frozen Isicles
Like Jewels round about my head, to cool me;
My eyes burn out, and sink into their sockets,
And my infected brain like brimstone boils,
I live in Hell, and several furies vex me;
O carry me where no Sun ever shew'd yet
A face of comfort, where the earth is Crystal,
Never to be dissolv'd, where naught inhabits
But night and cold, and nipping frosts, and winds
That cut the stubborn rocks and make them shiver;
Set me there friends.

RUGIO
Hold fast, he must to bed, Fryer, what scalding sweats he has!

MARCO
He'll scald in Hell for't, that was the cause.

ALPHONSO
Drink, drink, a world of drink,
Fill all the cups and all the antick vessels,
And borrow pots, let me have drink enough,
Bring all the worthy drunkards of the time,
The experienc'd drunkards, let me have them all,
And let them drink their worst, I'le make them Ideots,
I'le lye upon my Back and swallow Vessels;
Have Rivers made of cooling Wine run through me,
Not stay for this mans health, or this great Princes,

But take an Ocean, and begin to all; Oh, oh.

MARCO
He cools a little, now away with him,
And to his warm bed presently.

ALPHONSO
No drink? no wind? no cooling air?

RUGIO
You shall have any thing.
His hot fit lessens, Heaven put in a hand now,
And save his life; there's drink Sir in your chamber,
And all cool things.

ALPHONSO
Away, away, let's fly to 'em.

[Exeunt.

[Enter **VALERIO** and **EVANTHE**.

EVANTHE
To say you were impotent, I am asham'd on't,
To make your self no man, to a fresh Maid too,
A longing Maid, upon her wedding night also,
To give her such a dor.

VALERIO
I prethee pardon me.

EVANTHE
Had you been drunk, 't had been excusable,
Or like a Gentleman under the Surgions hands,
And so not able, there had been some colour,
But wretchedly to take a weakness to ye,
A fearful weakness, to abuse your body,
And let a lye work like a spell upon ye,
A lye, to save your life.

VALERIO
Will you give me leave, sweet?

EVANTHE
You have taken too much leave, and too base leave too,
To wrong your love; hast thou a noble spirit?
And canst thou look up to the peoples loves,
That call thee worthy, and not blush, Valerio?

Canst thou behold me that thou hast betray'd thus,
And no shame touch thee?

VALERIO
Shame attend the sinful, I know my innocence.

EVANTHE
Ne'r think to face it, that's a double weakness,
And shews thee falser still; the King himself,
Though he be wicked, and our Enemy,
But juster than thou art, in pity of my injuries,
Told me the truth.

VALERIO
What did he tell thee, Evanthe?

EVANTHE
That but to gain thy life a fortnight longer,
Thy lov'd poor life, thou gav'st up all my duties.

VALERIO
I swear 'tis false; my life and death are equal,
I have weigh'd 'em both, and find 'em but one fortune,
But Kings are men, and live as men, and dye too,
Have the affections men have, and their falsehoods;
Indeed they have more power to make 'em good;
The King's to blame, it was to save thy life Wench,
Thy innocent life, that I forbore thy bed,
For if I had toucht thee thou hadst dyed, he swore it.

EVANTHE
And was not I as worthy to dye nobly?
To make a story for the time that follows,
As he that married me? what weakness, Sir,
Or disability do you see in me,
Either in mind or body? to defraud me
Of such an opportunity? Do you think I married you
Only for pleasure, or content in lust?
To lull you in my arms, and kiss you hourly?
Was this my end? I might have been a Queen, Sir,
If that had caught me, and have known all delicates;
There's few that would have shun'd so fair an offer.
O thou unfaithful fearful man, thou hast kill'd me,
In saving me this way, thou hast destroy'd me,
Rob'd me of that thy love can never give more;
To be unable to save me? O misery!
Had I been my Valerio, thou Evanthe,
I would have lyen with thee under a Gallows,

Though the Hangman had been my Hymen, and the furies
With iron whips and forks, ready to torture me.
I would have hug'd thee too, though Hell had gap'd at me;
Save my life! that expected to dye bravely,
That would have woo'd it too: Would I had married
An Eunuch, that had truly no ability,
Then such a fearful lyar, thou hast done me
A scurvy courtesie, that has undone me.

VALERIO

I'le do no more, since you are so nobly fashion'd,
Made up so strongly, I'le take my share with ye,
Nay, dear, I'le learn of you.

EVANTHE

He weeps too tenderly;
My anger's gone, good my Lord pardon me,
And if I have offended, be more angry,
It was a Womans flash, a sudden valour,
That could not lye conceal'd.

VALERIO

I honour ye, by all the rites of holy marriage,
And pleasures of chaste love, I wonder at ye,
You appear the vision of a Heaven unto me,
Stuck all with stars of honour shining clearly,
And all the motions of your mind Celestial;
Man is a lump of Earth, the best man spiritless,
To such a woman; all our lives and actions
But counterfeits in Arras to this vertue;
Chide me again, you have so brave an anger,
And flows so nobly from you, thus deliver'd,
That I could suffer like a Child to hear ye,
Nay make my self guilty of some faults to honour ye.

EVANTHE

I'le chide no more, you have rob'd me of my courage,
And with a cunning patience checkt my impudence;
Once more forgiveness?

[She kneels.

VALERIO

Will this serve, Evanthe?

[Kisses her.

And this my love? Heavens mercy be upon us;

But did he tell no more?

EVANTHE
Only this trifle: you set my woman on me, to betray me;
'Tis true, she did her best, a bad old woman,
It stir'd me, Sir.

VALERIO
I cannot blame thee, Jewel.

EVANTHE
And me thought when your name was sounded that way—

VALERIO
He that will spare no fame, will spare no name, sweet;
Though as I am a man, I am full of weakness,
And may slip happily into some ignorance,
Yet at my years to be a bawd, and cozen
Mine own hopes with my Doctrine—

EVANTHE
I believe not, nor never shall; our time is out to morrow.

VALERIO
Let's be to night then full of fruitfulness,
Now we are both of one mind, let's be happy,
I am no more a wanting man, Evanthe,
Thy warm embraces shall dissolve that impotence,
And my cold lye shall vanish with thy kisses;
You hours of night be long, as when Alcmena
Lay by the lusty side of Jupiter;
Keep back the day, and hide his golden beams,
Where the chaste watchful morning may not find 'em;
Old doting Tython hold Aurora fast,
And though she blush the day-break from her cheeks,
Conceal her still; thou heavy Wain stand firm,
And stop the quicker revolutions;
Or if the day must come, to spoil our happiness,
Thou envious Sun peep not upon our pleasure,
Thou that all Lovers curse, be far off from us.

[Enter **CASTRUCHIO** with **GUARD**.

EVANTHE
Then let's to bed, and this night in all joyes
And chaste delights—

CASTRUCHIO

Stay, I must part ye both;
It is the Kings command, who bids me tell ye,
To morrow is your last hour.

VALERIO
I obey, Sir,
In Heaven we shall meet, Captain, where King Frederick
Dare not appear to part us.

CASTRUCHIO
Mistake me not, though I am rough in doing of my Office,
You shall find, Sir, you have a friend to honour ye.

VALERIO
I thank ye, Sir.

EVANTHE
Pray captain tell the King,
They that are sad on Earth, in Heaven shall sing.

[Exeunt.

ACTUS QUINTUS

SCÆNA PRIMA

Enter Friar **MARCO** and **RUGIO**.

RUGIO
Have you writ to the Captain of the Castle?

MARCO
Yes, and charged him
Upon his souls health, that he be not cruel,
Told him Valerio's worth among the people,
And how it must be punisht in posterity,
Though he scape now.

RUGIO
But will not he, Fryer Marco, betray this to the King?

MARCO
Though he be stubborn, and of a rugged nature, yet he is honest,
And honours much Valerio.

RUGIO

How does Alphonso?
For now me thinks my heart is light again,
And pale fear fled.

MARCO
He is as well as I am;
The Rogue against his will has sav'd his life,
A desperate poison has re-cur'd the Prince.

RUGIO
To me 'tis most miraculous.

MARCO
To me too, till I consider why it should do so,
And now I have found it a most excellent Physick,
It wrought upon the dull cold misty parts,
That clog'd his soul, which was another poison,
A desperate too, and found such matter there,
And such abundance also to resist it,
And wear away the dangerous heat it brought with it,
The pure blood and the spirits scap'd untainted.

RUGIO
'Twas Heavens high hand, none of Sorano's pity.

MARCO
Most certain 'twas, had the malitious villain

[Enter **CASTRUCHIO**.

Given him a cooling poison, he had paid him.

RUGIO
The Captain of the Castle.

MARCO
O ye are welcome, how does your Prisoner?

CASTRUCHIO
He must go for dead;
But when I do a deed of so much villany,
I'le have my skin pull'd o're mine ears, my Lord,

[Enter **ALPHONSO** and **FRIARS**.

Though I am the Kings, I am none of his abuses;
How does your Royal charge? that I might see once.

MARCO

I pray see now, you are a trusty Gentleman.

ALPHONSO

Good Fathers, I thank Heaven, I feel no sickness.

CASTRUCHIO

He speaks again.

ALPHONSO

Nothing that bars the free use of my spirit,
Me thinks the air's sweet to me, and company
A thing I covet now, Castruchio.

CASTRUCHIO

Sir, he speaks, and knows, for Heaven sake break my pate Lord,
That I may be sure I sleep not.

ALPHONSO

Thou wert honest,
Ever among the rank of good men counted,
I have been absent long out of the world,
A dream I have lived, how does it look Castruchio?
What wonders are abroad?

CASTRUCHIO

I fling off duty to your dead Brother, for he is dead in goodness,
And to the living hope of brave Alphonso,
The noble heir of nature, and of honour,
I fasten my Allegeance.

MARCO

Softly Captain, we dare not trust the Air with this blest secret,
Good Sir, be close again, Heaven has restor'd ye,
And by miraculous means, to your fair health,
And made the instrument your enemies malice,
Which does prognosticate your noble fortune;
Let not our careless joy lose you again, Sir,
Help to deliver ye to a further danger,
I pray you pass in, and rest a while forgotten,
For if your Brother come to know you are well again,
And ready to inherit as your right,
Before we have strength enough to assure your life,
What will become of you? and what shall we
Deserve in all opinions that are honest,
For our loss of judgment, care, and loyalty?

RUGIO

Dear Sir, pass in, Heaven has begun the work,
And blest us all, let our indeavours follow,
To preserve this blessing to our timely uses,
And bring it to the noble end we aim at;
Let our cares work now, and our eyes pick out
An hour to shew ye safely to your Subjects,
A secure hour.

ALPHONSO
I am counsel'd; ye are faithful.

CASTRUCHIO
Which hour shall not be long, as we shall handle it.
Once more the tender of my duty.

ALPHONSO
Thank ye.

CASTRUCHIO
Keep you the Monastery.

RUGIO
Strong enough I'le warrant ye.

[Exeunt.

[Enter the **FOOL** and **PODRAMO**.

PODRAMO
Who are all these that crowd about the Court, Fool?
Those strange new faces?

FOOL
They are Suitors, Coxcomb,
Dainty fine Suitors to the Widow Lady,
Thou hadst best make one of 'em, thou wilt be hang'd as handsomly
At the Months end, and as much joy follow'd,
And 'twere to morrow; as many mourning Bawds for thee,
And holy Nuns, whose vestal fire ne'r vanishes,
In sackcloth Smocks, as if thou wert Heir apparent
To all the impious Suburbs, and the sink-holes.

PODRAMO
Out you base Rogue.

FOOL
Why dost abuse thy self?
Thou art to blame, I take thee for a Gentleman,

But why does not thy Lord and Master marry her?

PODRAMO
Why, she is his Sister.

FOOL
'Tis the better, Fool,
He may make bold with his own flesh and blood,
For o' my conscience there's none else will trust him;
Then he may pleasure the King at a dead pinch too,
Without a Mephestophilus, such as thou art,
And ingross the Royal disease like a true Subject.

PODRAMO
Thou wilt be whipt.

FOOL
I am sure thou wilt be hang'd,
I have lost a Ducket else, which I would be loth to venture
Without certainty. They appear.

[**SUITORS** pass by.

PODRAMO
Why these are Rascals.

FOOL
They were meant to be so, does thy Master deserve
better kindred?

PODRAMO
There's an old Lawyer,
Trim'd up like a Gally Foist, what would he do with her?

FOOL
As Usurers do with their Gold, he would look on her,
And read her over once a day, like a hard report,
Feed his dull eye, and keep his fingers itching;
For any thing else, she may appeal to a Parliament,
Sub Poena's and Post Kaes have spoil'd his Codpiece;
There's a Physician too, older than he,
And Gallen Gallinacius, but he has lost his spurs,
He would be nibling too.

PODRAMO
I marked the man, if he be a man.

FOOL

H'as much ado to be so,
Searcloths and Sirrups glew him close together,
He would fall a pieces else; mending of she Patients,
And then trying whether they be right or no
In his own person, there's the honest care on't,
Has mollifi'd the man; if he do marry her,
And come but to warm him well at Cupids Bonfire,
He will bulge so subtilly and suddenly,
You may snatch him up by parcels, like a Sea Rack:
Will your Worship go, and look upon the rest, Sir?
And hear what they can say for themselves.

PODRAMO
I'le follow thee.

[Exeunt.

[Enter **CAMILLO**, **MENALLO**, **CLEANTHES**, and **CASTRUCHIO**.

CAMILLO
You tell us wonders.

CASTRUCHIO
But I tell you truths, they are both well.

MENALLO
Why are not we in Arms then?
And all the Island given to know—

CASTRUCHIO
Discreetly and privately it must be done, 'twill miss else,
And prove our ruines; most of the noble Citizens
Know it by me, and stay the hour to attend it,
Prepare your hearts and friends, let their's be right too,
And keep about the King to avoid suspicion;

[Enter **FREDERICK** and **SORANO**.

When you shall hear the Castle Bell, take courage,
And stand like men, away, the King is coming.

[Exeunt **LORDS**.

FREDERICK
Now Captain, what have you done with your prisoner?

CASTRUCHIO
He is dead, Sir, and his body flung into the Sea,

To feed the fishes, 'twas your will, I take it,
I did it from a strong Commission,
And stood not to capitulate.

FREDERICK
'Tis well done,
And I shall love you for your faith. What anger
Or sorrow did he utter at his end?

CASTRUCHIO
Faith little, Sir, that I gave any ear to,
He would have spoke, but I had no Commission
To argue with him, so I flung him off;
His Lady would have seen, but I lockt her up,
For fear her womans tears should hinder us.

FREDERICK
'Twas trusty still. I wonder, my Sorano,
We hear not from the Monastery; I believe
They gave it not, or else it wrought not fully.

CASTRUCHIO
Did you name the Monastery?

FREDERICK
Yes, I did Captain.

CASTRUCHIO
I saw the Fryer this morning, and Lord Rugio,
Bitterly weeping, and wringing of their hands,
And all the holy men hung down their heads.

SORANO
'Tis done I'le warrant ye.

CASTRUCHIO
I ask'd the reason.

FREDERICK
What answer hadst thou?

CASTRUCHIO
This in few words, Sir,
Your Brother's dead, this morning he deceased,
I was your servant, and I wept not, Sir,
I knew 'twas for your good.

FREDERICK

It shall be for thine too,
Captain, indeed it shall. O my Sorano,
Now we shall live.

SORANO
I, now there's none to trouble ye.

FREDERICK
Captain, bring out the woman, and give way
To any Suitor that shall come to marry her,
Of what degree soever.

CASTRUCHIO
It shall be done, Sir.

[Exit **CASTRUCHIO**.

FREDERICK
O let me have a lusty Banquet after it,

[Enter **EVANTHE, CAMILLO, CLEANTHES, MENALLO, FOOL.**

I will be high and merry.

SORANO
There be some Lords
That I could counsel ye to fling from Court, Sir,
They pry into our actions, they are such
The foolish people call their Countries honours,
Honest brave things, and stile them with such Titles,
As if they were the patterns of the Kingdom,
Which makes them proud, and prone to look into us,
And talk at random of our actions,
They should be lovers of your commands,
And followers of your will; bridles and curbs
To the hard headed Commons that malign us,
They come here to do honour to my Sister,
To laugh at your severity, and fright us;
If they had power, what would these men do?
Do you hear, Sir, how privily they whisper?

FREDERICK
I shall silence 'em,
And to their shames within this week Sorano,
In the mean time have patience.

SORANO
How they jeer, and look upon me as I were a Monster!

And talk and jeer! how I shall pull your plumes, Lords
How I shall humble ye within these two daies!
Your great names, nor your Country cannot save ye.

FREDERICK
Let in the Suitors. Yet submit, I'le pardon ye,
You are half undone already, do not wind
My anger to that height, it may consume ye,

[Enter **LAWYER, PHYSICIAN, CAPTAIN, CUT-PURSE.**

And utterly destroy thee, fair Evanthe: yet I have mercy.

EVANTHE
Use it to your bawds,
To me use cruelty, it best becomes ye,
And shews more Kingly: I contemn your mercy,
It is a cozening, and a bawdy mercy;
Can any thing be hoped for, to relieve me?
Or is it fit? I thank you for a pity, when you have kill'd my Lord.

FREDERICK
Who will have her?

EVANTHE
My tears are gone,
My tears of love to my dear Valerio,
But I have fill'd mine eyes again with anger;
O were it but so powerful to consume ye.
My tongue with curses I have arm'd against ye,
With Maiden curses, that Heaven crowns with horrors,
My heart set round with hate against thy tyranny;
O would my hands could hold the fire of Heaven,
Wrapt in the thunder that the Gods revenge with,
That like stern Justice I might fling it on thee;
Thou art a King of Monsters, not of men,
And shortly thou wilt turn this Land to Devils.

FREDERICK
I'le make you one first, and a wretched Devil,
Come who will have her?

LAWYER
I an't like your Majesty, I am a Lawyer,
I can make her a Joynture of any mans Land in Naples,
And she shall keep it too, I have a trick for it.

FOOL

Canst thou make her a Joynture of thine honesty?
Or thy ability, thou lewd abridgment?
Those are non suted and flung o're the bar.

PHYSICIAN
An't please your Majesty to give me leave,
I dare accept her; and though old I seem, Lady,
Like Æson, by my art I can renew youth and ability.

FOOL
In a powdering Tub
Stew thy self tender again, like a Cock Chicken,
The broth may be good, but the flesh is not fit for dogs sure.

CAPTAIN
Lady, take me, and I'le maintain thine honour,
I am a poor Captain, as poor people call me,
Very poor people, for my Souldiers
They are quartered in the outside of the City,
Men of ability, to make good a high way;
We have but two grand Enemies that oppose us,
The Don Gout, and the Gallows.

FOOL
I believe ye, and both these you will bind her for a Jointure;
Now Signior firk.

CUT-PURSE
Madam, take me and be wise,
I am rich and nimble, and those are rare in one man,
Every mans pocket is my Treasury,
And no man wears a Sute but fits me neatly;
Cloaths you shall have, and wear the purest Linnen,
I have a tribute out of every Shop, Lady,
Meat you shall eat, I have my Caters out too,
The best and lustiest, and drink good Wine, good Lady,
Good quickening Wine, Wine that will make you caper.
And at the worst—

FOOL
It is but capering short, Sir,
You seldom stay for Agues or for Surfeits,
A shaking fit of a whip sometimes o'retakes ye,
Marry you dye most commonly of choakings,
Obstructions of the halter are your ends ever;
Pray leave your horn and your knife for her to live on.

EVANTHE

Poor wretched people, why do you wrong your selves?
Though I fear'd death, I should fear you ten times more,
You are every one a new death, and an odious,
The earth will purifie corrupted bodies,
You'll make us worse and stink eternally.
Go home, go home and get good Nurses for you,
Dream not of Wives.

FREDERICK
You shall have one of 'em, if they dare venture for ye.

EVANTHE
They are dead already,
Crawling diseases that must creep into
The next grave they find open, are these fit Husbands
For her you have loved, Sir? though you hate me now,
And hate me mortally, as I hate you,
Your nobleness, in that you have done otherwise,
And named Evanthe once as your poor Mistris,
Might offer worthier choice.

FREDERICK
Speak, who dare take her for one moneth, and then dye?

PHYSICIAN
Dye, Sir?

FREDERICK
I, dye Sir, that's the condition.

PHYSICIAN
One moneth is too little
For me to repent in for my former pleasure,
To go still on, unless I were sure she would kill me,
And kill me delicately before my day,
Make it up a year, for by that time I must dye,
My body will hold out no longer.

FREDERICK
No Sir, it must be but a moneth.

LAWYER
Then farewel Madam,
This is like to be a great year of dissention
Among good people, and I dare not lose it,
There will be money got.

CAPTAIN

Bless your good Ladiship, there's nothing in the
grave but bones and ashes,
In Taverns there's good wine, and excellent wenches,
And Surgeons while we live.

CUT-PURSE
Adieu sweet Lady,
Lay me when I am dead near a rich Alderman,
I cannot pick his Purse, no, I'le no dying,
Though I steal Linnen, I'le not steal my shrowd yet.

ALL
Send ye a happy match.

[Exeunt.

FOOL
And you all halters, you have deserved 'em richly.
These do all Villanies, and mischiefs of all sorts, yet those they fear not,
To flinch where a fair wench is at the stake.

EVANTHE
Come, your sentence, let me dye: you see, Sir,
None of your valiant men dare venture on me,
A Moneth's a dangerous thing.

[Enter **VALERIO** disguis'd.

FREDERICK
Away with her, let her dye instantly.

EVANTHE
Will you then be willing
To dye at the time prefixt? that I must know too,
And know it beyond doubt.

FREDERICK
What if I did wench?

EVANTHE
On that condition if I had it certain,
I would be your any thing, and you should injoy me,
How ever in my nature I abhor you,
Yet as I live I would be obedient to you;
But when your time came how I should rejoyce,
How then I should bestir my self to thank ye,
To see your throat cut, how my heart would leap, Sir!
I would dye with you, but first I would so torture ye,

And cow you in your end, so despise you,
For a weak and wretched coward, you must end sure;
Still make ye fear, and shake, despised, still laugh at ye.

FREDERICK
Away with her, let her dye instantly.

CAMILLO
Stay, there's another, and a Gentleman,
His habit shews no less, may be his business
Is for this Ladies love.

FREDERICK
Say why ye come, Sir, and what you are.

VALERIO
I am descended nobly, a Prince by birth, and by my trade
a Souldier,
A Princes fellow, Abidos brought me forth,
My Parents Duke Agenor, and fair Egla,
My business hither to renew my love
With a young noble spirit, call'd Valerio;
Our first acquaintance was at Sea, in fight
Against a Turkish man of War, a stout one,
Where Lyon-like I saw him shew his valour,
And as he had been made of compleat vertue,
Spirit, and fire, no dregs of dull earth in him.

EVANTHE
Thou art a brave Gentleman, and bravely speakest him.

VALERIO
The Vessel dancing under him for joy,
And the rough whistling winds becalm'd to view him;
I saw the child of honour, for he was young,
Deal such an Alms amongst the spightful Pagans,
His towring sword flew like an eager Falkon,
And round about his reach invade the Turks,
He had intrencht himself in his dead quarries;
The silver Crescents on the tops they carried
Shrunk in their heads to see his rage so bloody,
And from his fury suffered sad eclipses;
The game of death was never plaid more nobly,
The meager thief grew wanton in his mischiefs,
And his shrunk hollow eyes smil'd on his ruines.

EVANTHE
Heaven keep this Gentleman from being a Suitor,

For I shall ne'r deny him, he's so noble.

VALERIO
But what can last long? strength and spirit wasted,
And fresh supplies flew on upon this Gentleman,
Breathless and weary with oppression,
And almost kill'd with killing, 'twas my chance
In a tall Ship I had to view the fight;
I set into him, entertain'd the Turk,
And for an hour gave him so hot a breakfast,
He clapt all linnen up he had to save him,
And like a Lovers thought he fled our fury;
There first I saw the man I lov'd, Valerio,
There was acquainted, there my soul grew to him,
And his to me, we were the twins of friendship.

EVANTHE
Fortune protect this man, or I shall ruine him.

VALERIO
I made this voyage to behold my friend,
To warm my love anew at his affection;
But since I landed, I have heard his fate:
My Father's had not been to me more cruel,
I have lamented too, and yet I keep
The treasure of a few tears for you Lady,
For by description you were his Evanthe.

EVANTHE
Can he weep that's a stranger to my story?
And I stand still and look on? Sir, I thank ye;
If noble spirits after their departure,
Can know, and wish, certain his soul gives thanks too;
There are your tears again, and when yours fail, Sir,
Pray ye call to me, I have some store to lend ye. Your name?

VALERIO
Urbino.

EVANTHE
That I may remember,
That little time I have to live, your friendships,
My tongue shall study both.

FREDERICK
Do you come hither, only to tell this story, Prince Urbino?

VALERIO

My business now is, Sir, to woo this Lady.

EVANTHE
Blessing defend ye; do you know the danger?

VALERIO
Yes, and I fear it not, danger's my play-fellow,
Since I was man 'thas been my best companion,
I know your doom, 'tis for a Moneth you give her,
And then his life you take that marries her.

FREDERICK
'Tis true, nor can your being born a Prince,
If you accept the offer, free you from it.

VALERIO
I not desire it, I have cast the worst,
And even that worst to me is many blessings;
I lov'd my friend, not measur'd out by time,
Nor hired by circumstance of place and honour,
But for his wealthy self and worth I lov'd him,
His mind and noble mold he ever mov'd in,
And wooe his friend because she was worthy of him,
The only relique that he left behind, Sir;
To give his ashes honour, Lady take me,
And in me keep Valerio's love alive still,
When I am gone, take those that shall succeed me,
Heaven must want light, before you want a Husband,
To raise up heirs of love and noble memory,
To your unfortunate—

EVANTHE
Am I still hated? hast thou no end, O fate, of my affliction?
Was I ordain'd to be a common Murdress?
And of the best men too? Good Sir—

VALERIO
Peace Sweet, look on my hand.

EVANTHE
I do accept the Gentleman, I faint with joy.

FREDERICK
I stop it, none shall have her, convey this stranger hence.

VALERIO
I am no stranger—Hark to the bell, that rings,
Hark, hark, proud Frederick, that was King of mischief,

Hark, thou abhorred man, dost thou hear thy sentence?
Does not this bell ring in thine ears thy ruine?

FREDERICK
What bell is this?

CAMILLO
The Castle bell: Stand sure, Sir, and move not, if you
do you perish.

MENALLO
It rings your knell; Alphonso, King Alphonso.

ALL
Alphonso, King Alphonso.

FREDERICK
I am betrai'd, lock fast the Palace.

CAMILLO
We have all the keys, Sir.
And no door here shall shut without our Licence.

CLEANTHES
Do you shake now, Lord Sorano? no new trick?
Nor speedy poison to prevent this business?
No bawdy meditation now to fly to?

FREDERICK
Treason, Treason, Treason.

CAMILLO
Yes, we hear ye,

[Enter **ALPHONSO, RUGIO, MARCO, CASTRUCHIO, QUEEN** with **GUARD**.

And we have found the Traytor in your shape, Sir,
We'll keep him fast too.

FREDERICK
Recover'd! then I am gone,
The Sun of all my pomp is set and vanisht.

ALPHONSO
Have you not forgot this face of mine, King Frederick?
Brother, I am come to see you, and have brought
A Banquet to be merry with your Grace;
I pray sit down, I do beseech your Majesty,

And eat, eat freely, Sir, why do you start?
Have you no stomach to the meat I bring you?
Dare you not taste? have ye no Antidotes?
You need not fear; Sorano's a good Apothecary,
Me thinks you look not well, some fresh wine for him,
Some of the same he sent me by Sorano;
I thank you for't, it sav'd my life, I am bound to ye,
But how 'twill work on you—I hope your Lordship
Will pledge him too, me thinks you look but scurvily,
And would be put into a better colour,
But I have a candi'd Toad for your Lordship.

SORANO
Would I had any thing that would dispatch me,
So it were down, and I out of this fear once.

FREDERICK
Sir, Thus low as my duty now compells me,
I do confess my unbounded sins, my errours,
And feel within my soul the smarts already;
Hide not the noble nature of a Brother,
The pity of a friend, from my afflictions;
Let me a while lament my misery,
And cast the load off of my wantonness,
Before I find your fury, then strike home,
I do deserve the deepest blow of Justice,
And then how willingly, O death, I'le meet thee!

ALPHONSO
Rise, Madam, those sweet tears are potent speakers,
And Brother live, but in the Monastery,
Where I lived, with the self same silence too,
I'le teach you to be good against your will, Brother,
Your tongue has done much harm, that must be dumb now;
The daily pilgrimage to my Fathers Tomb,
Tears, sighs, and groans, you shall wear out your daies with,
And true ones too, you shall perform dear Brother;
Your diet shall be slender to inforce these; too light a penance, Sir.

FREDERICK
I do confess it.

ALPHONSO
Sorano you shall—

SORANO
How he studies for it!
Hanging's the least part of my penance certain.

[**EVANTHE** Kneels.

ALPHONSO
What Lady's that that kneels?

CASTRUCHIO
The chaste Evanthe.

ALPHONSO
Sweet, your Petition?

EVANTHE
'Tis for this bad man, Sir,
Abominable bad, but yet my Brother.

ALPHONSO
The bad man shall attend as bad a Master,
And both shall be confin'd within the Monastery;
His rank flesh shall be pull'd with daily fasting,
But once a week he shall smell meat, he will surfeit else,
And his immodest mind, compell'd to prayer;
On the bare boards he shall lye, to remember
The wantonness he did commit in beds;
And drink fair water, that will ne'r inflame him;
He sav'd my life, though he purpos'd to destroy me,
For which I'le save his, though I make it miserable:
Madam, at Court I shall desire your company,
You are wise and vertuous, when you please to visit
My Brother Frederick, you shall have our Licence,
My dear best friend, Valerio.

VALERIO
Save Alphonso.

OMNES
Long live Alphonso, King of us, and Naples.

ALPHONSO
Is this the Lady that the wonder goes on?
Honour'd sweet Maid, here take her my Valerio,
The King now gives her, she is thine own without fear:
Brother, have you so much provision that is good?
Not season'd by Sorano and his Cooks?
That we may venture on with honest safety,
We and our friends?

FREDERICK

All that I have is yours, Sir.

ALPHONSO
Come then, let's in, and end this Nuptial,
Then to our Coronation with all speed:
My vertuous Maid, this day I'le be your Bride-man,
And see you bedded to your own desires too;
Beshrew me Lords, who is not merry hates me,
Only Sorano shall not bear my cup:
Come, now forget old pains and injuries,
As I must do, and drown all in fair healths;
That Kingdom's blessed, where the King begins
His true love first, for there all loves are twins.

[Exeunt **OMNES**.

EPILOGUE

We have your favours, Gentlemen, and you
Have our indeavours, (dear Friends grudge not now,)
There's none of you, but when you please can sell
Many a lame Horse, and many a fair tale tell;
Can put off many a Maid unto a friend,
That was not so since th' action at Mile-end;
Ours is a Virgin yet, and they that love
Untainted flesh, we hope our friends will prove.

John Fletcher – A Short Biography

John Fletcher was born in December, 1579 in Rye, Sussex. He was baptised on December 20th.

As can be imagined details of much of his life and career have not survived and, accordingly, only a very brief indication of his life and works can be given.

His father, Richard Fletcher, was a successful and rather ambitious cleric. From being the Dean of Peterborough he moved on to become the Bishop of Bristol, Bishop of Worcester and finally, shortly before his death, the Bishop of London. He was also the chaplain to Queen Elizabeth.

When he was Dean of Peterborough, Richard Fletcher, witnessed the execution of Mary, Queen of Scots. It was said he "knelt down on the scaffold steps and started to pray out loud and at length, in a prolonged and rhetorical style, as though determined to force his way into the pages of history". He cried out at her death, "So perish all the Queen's enemies!" All very dramatic but the family did have strong links to the Arts.

Young Fletcher appears at the very young age of eleven to have entered Corpus Christi College at Cambridge University in 1591. There are no records that he ever took a degree but there is some small evidence that he was being prepared for a career in the church.

However what is clear is that this was soon abandoned as he joined the stream of people who would leave University and decamp to the more bohemian life of commercial theatre in London.

Unfortunately his father fell out with Queen Elizabeth but appears to have been on his way to rehabilitation before his death in 1596. At his death he was, however, mired in debt.

The upbringing of the now teenage Fletcher and his seven siblings now passed to his paternal uncle, the poet and minor official Giles Fletcher. Giles, who had the patronage of the Earl of Essex may have been a liability rather than an advantage to the young Fletcher. With Essex involved in the failed rebellion against Elizabeth Giles was also tainted by association.

By 1606 John Fletcher appears to have equipped himself with the talents to become a playwright. Initially this appears to have been for the Children of the Queen's Revels, then performing at the Blackfriars Theatre.

Commendatory verses by Richard Brome in the Beaumont and Fletcher 1647 folio place Fletcher in the company of Ben Jonson, although it is not known when this friendship began. Jonson, of course, was a leviathan of English Literature, so admired that many of his literary friends and colleagues were simply known as 'Sons of Ben'. Fletcher's frequent early collaborator, Francis Beaumont, was also a friend of Jonson's.

Fletcher's early career was marked by one significant failure; The Faithful Shepherdess, his adaptation of Giovanni Battista Guarini's Il Pastor Fido, which was performed by the Blackfriars Children in 1608. In the preface to the printed edition of his play, Fletcher explained the failure as due to his audience's faulty expectations. They expected a pastoral tragicomedy to feature dances, comedy, and murder, with the shepherds presented in conventional stereotypes – as Fletcher put it, wearing "gray cloaks, with curtailed dogs in strings." Fletcher's preface is however best known for its pithy definition of tragicomedy: "A tragicomedy is not so called in respect of mirth and killing, but in respect it wants [i.e., lacks] deaths, which is enough to make it no tragedy; yet brings some near it, which is enough to make it no comedy." A comedy, he went on to say, must be "a representation of familiar people." His preface is critical of drama that features characters whose action violates nature.

In that case, Fletcher appears to have been developing a new style faster than audiences could comprehend. By 1609, however, he had found his stride. With Beaumont, he wrote Philaster, which became a hit for the King's Men and began a profitable association between Fletcher and that company. Philaster appears also to have begun a trend for tragicomedy. Fletcher's influence has also been said to have inspired some features of Shakespeare's late romances, and certainly his influence on the tragicomic work of other playwrights is even more marked.

By the middle of the 1610s, Fletcher's plays had achieved a popularity that rivalled Shakespeare's and cemented the pre-eminence of the King's Men in Jacobean London. After Beaumont's retirement, necessitated by ill-health, and then his early death in 1616, Fletcher continued working, both singly and in collaboration, until his death in 1625. By that time, he had produced, or had been credited with, close to fifty plays. This body of work remained a major part of the King's Men's repertory until the closing of the theatres in 1642 due to the Civil War.

At the beginning of his career Fletcher's most important collaborator was Francis Beaumont. The two wrote together for close to a decade, first for the Children of the Queen's Revels, and then for the King's Men. According to an anecdote transmitted or invented by John Aubrey, they also lived together in Bankside, sharing clothes and having "one wench in the house between them." This domestic arrangement, if it existed, was ended by Beaumont's marriage in 1613, and their dramatic partnership ended after Beaumont fell ill, probably of a stroke, that same year.

At this point Fletcher had written many plays with Beaumont and several others on his own. He seems to have been regarded as quite a talent although it should be remembered that playwrights were required to be prolific, to easily work with other collaborators and to produce work of quality and commercial appeal very quickly.

The King's Men, run by Philip Henslowe, was the most prestigious of the theatre companies and Fletcher now had an increasingly close association with it.

Fletcher collaborated with Shakespeare on Henry VIII, The Two Noble Kinsmen, and the now lost Cardenio, which some scholars say was the basis for Lewis Theobald's play Double Falsehood. (Theobald is regarded as one of the best Shakespearean editors. Whether his play is based on Cardenio or on some other is not absolutely known although Theobald certainly promoted it as his revision of the lost Shakespeare/Fletcher play.)

A play that Fletcher also wrote by himself at this time, The Woman's Prize or the Tamer Tamed, is also regarded as a sequel to The Taming of the Shrew.

In 1616, with the death of Shakespeare, Fletcher now appears to have entered into an enhanced arrangement with the King's Men on very similar terms to Shakespeare's. Fletcher would now write exclusively for the King's Men until his own death almost a decade later.

As well as continuing his solo productions Fletcher was still collaborating with other playwrights, mainly Philip Massinger, who, in turn, would succeed him as the in-house playwright for the King's Men.

Fletcher's popularity continued throughout his life; indeed during the winter of 1621, he had three of his plays performed at court. His mastery is most notable in two dramatic types; tragicomedy and the comedy of manners.

John Fletcher died in 1625, it is thought of bubonic plague which, at the time, was undergoing further outbreaks.

He seems to have been buried in what is now Southwark Cathedral, although a precise location is not known. There is much made of an anecdote that Fletcher and Massinger (who died in 1640) share the same grave but it is more likely that both are buried within a few yards of each other and that the stone markers in the floor have confused the issue. One is marked 'Edmond Shakespeare 1607' and the other 'John Fletcher 1625' refers to Shakespeare's younger brother and the playwright. The churchyards were, more often than not, completely over-crowded and breeding grounds for disease. Precise record keeping was not a practiced skill.

During the later Commonwealth, many of the playwright's best-known scenes were kept alive as drolls. These were brief performances, usually condensed into one or two scenes and with the addition of music or song to satisfy the taste for plays while the theatres were closed under the Puritians. At the re-opening of the theatres in 1660, the plays in the Fletcher canon, in original form or revised, were by far the most common productions on the English stage. The most frequently revived plays suggest the developing taste for comedies of manners. Among the tragedies, The Maid's Tragedy and, especially, Rollo Duke of Normandy held the stage. Four tragicomedies (A King and No King, The Humorous Lieutenant, Philaster, and The Island Princess) were popular, perhaps in part for their similarity to and foreshadowing of heroic drama. Four comedies (Rule a Wife And Have a Wife, The Chances, Beggars' Bush, and especially The Scornful Lady) were also stage mainstays.

Despite his popularity, and it appears he was held in higher regard than Shakespeare at this time, his works steadily lost ground to those of Shakespeare and to new productions from other playwrights.

Since then Fletcher has increasingly become a subject only for occasional revivals and for specialists. Fletcher and his collaborators have been the subject of important bibliographic and critical studies, but the plays have been revived only infrequently.

Due to the frequent collaborations between all manner of playwrights, and the revisions carried out in later years, having a settled list of authorship to any given set of plays can be problematic. The works of Fletcher and others of this period most definitely fall into this category. It is as well to take into account that during this period theatres were quite often closed either due to outbreaks of the plague or to the prevailing political and moral climate. Printers, anxious to provide materials that would sell, were not above changing a name or two to enhance sales.

Although Fletcher collaborated most often with Beaumont and Massinger, it is believed that Massinger revised many of the plays some time after their original production. Other collaborators including Nathan Field, William Shakespeare, William Rowley and others also can be seen distinctly in Fletchers' works. Many modern scholars point out that Fletcher had many particular mannerisms but other playwrights would also duplicate these at times so allocating exact contributions of anyone to a play is somewhat of a detective case in many instances. However from the original folio printings or licensing via the Master of the Revels (the statutory licensing authority to approve and censor plays as well a hand in publication and printing of theatrical materials) as well as contemporary notes a fairly precise bibliography of the works can be given with only a few plays lacking substantial authority and provenance.

John Fletcher – A Concise Bibliography

This bibliography gives the most likely date of writing together with when published, revised or licensed by the Master or the Revels (This position within the royal household was originally for royal festivities, ie revels, and later to oversee stage censorship, until this function was transferred to the Lord Chamberlain in 1624).

Solo Plays
The Faithful Shepherdess, pastoral (written 1608–9; printed 1609)

The Tragedy of Valentinian, tragedy (1610–14; 1647)
Monsieur Thomas, comedy (c. 1610–16; 1639)
The Woman's Prize, or The Tamer Tamed, comedy (c. 1611; 1647)
Bonduca, tragedy (1611–14; 1647)
The Chances, comedy (c. 1613–25; 1647)
Wit Without Money, comedy (c. 1614; 1639)
The Mad Lover, tragicomedy (acted 5 January 1617; 1647)
The Loyal Subject, tragicomedy (licensed 16 November 1618; revised 1633; 1647)
The Humorous Lieutenant, tragicomedy (c. 1619; 1647)
Women Pleased, tragicomedy (c. 1619–23; 1647)
The Island Princess, tragicomedy (c. 1620; 1647)
The Wild Goose Chase, comedy (c. 1621; 1652)
The Pilgrim, comedy (c. 1621; 1647)
A Wife for a Month, tragicomedy (licensed 27 May 1624; 1647)
Rule a Wife and Have a Wife, comedy (licensed 19 October 1624; 1640)

Collaborations

With Francis Beaumont
The Woman Hater, comedy (1606; 1607)
Cupid's Revenge, tragedy (c. 1607–12; 1615)
Philaster, or Love Lies a-Bleeding, tragicomedy (c. 1609; 1620)
The Maid's Tragedy, Tragedy (c. 1609; 1619)
A King and No King, tragicomedy (1611; 1619)
The Captain, comedy (c. 1609–12; 1647)
The Scornful Lady, comedy (c. 1613; 1616)
Love's Pilgrimage, tragicomedy (c. 1615–16; 1647)
The Noble Gentleman, comedy (c. 1613; licensed 3 February 1626; 1647)

With Francis Beaumont & Philip Massinger
Thierry & Theodoret, tragedy (c. 1607; 1621)
The Coxcomb, comedy (c. 1608–10; 1647)
Beggars' Bush, comedy (c. 1612–13; revised 1622; 1647)
Love's Cure, comedy (c. 1612–13; revised 1625; 1647)

With Philip Massinger
Sir John van Olden Barnavelt, tragedy (August 1619; MS)
The Little French Lawyer, comedy (c. 1619–23; 1647)
A Very Woman, tragicomedy (c. 1619–22; licensed 6 June 1634; 1655)
The Custom of the Country, comedy (c. 1619–23; 1647)
The Double Marriage, tragedy (c. 1619–23; 1647)
The False One, history (c. 1619–23; 1647)
The Prophetess, tragicomedy (licensed 14 May 1622; 1647)
The Sea Voyage, comedy (licensed 22 June 1622; 1647)
The Spanish Curate, comedy (licensed 24 October 1622; 1647)
The Lovers' Progress or The Wandering Lovers, tragicomedy (licensed 6 December 1623; rev 1634; 1647)
The Elder Brother, comedy (c. 1625; 1637)

With Philip Massinger & Nathan Field
The Honest Man's Fortune, tragicomedy (1613; 1647)
The Queen of Corinth, tragicomedy (c. 1616–18; 1647)
The Knight of Malta, tragicomedy (c. 1619; 1647)

With William Shakespeare
Henry VIII, history (c. 1613; 1623)
The Two Noble Kinsmen, tragicomedy (c. 1613; 1634)
Cardenio, tragicomedy (c. 1613)

With Thomas Middleton & William Rowley
Wit at Several Weapons, comedy (c. 1610–20; 1647)

With William Rowley
The Maid in the Mill (licensed 29 August 1623; 1647).

With Nathan Field
Four Plays, or Moral Representations, in One, morality (c. 1608–13; 1647)

With Philip Massinger, Ben Jonson and George Chapman
Rollo Duke of Normandy, or The Bloody Brother, tragedy (c. 1617; revised 1627–30; 1639)

With James Shirley
The Night Walker, or The Little Thief, comedy (c. 1611; 1640)
The Coronation c. 1635

Uncertain
The Nice Valour, or The Passionate Madman, comedy (c. 1615–25; 1647)
The Laws of Candy, tragicomedy (c. 1619–23; 1647)
The Fair Maid of the Inn, comedy (licensed 22 January 1626; 1647)
The Faithful Friends, tragicomedy (registered 29 June 1660; MS.)

The Nice Valour is possibly by Fletcher revised by Thomas Middleton;

The Fair Maid of the Inn is perhaps a play by Massinger, John Ford, and John Webster, either with or without Fletcher's involvement.

The Laws of Candy has been variously attributed to Fletcher and to John Ford.

The Night-Walker was a Fletcher original, with additions by Shirley for a 1639 production.

Even now there is not absolute certainty on several of the plays. The first Beaumont & Fletcher folio of 1647 contained 35 plays and the second folio of 1679 added a further 18. In total 53 plays.

The first folio included The Masque of the Inner Temple and Gray's Inn (1613), and the second The Knight of the Burning Pestle (1607), widely considered Beaumont's solo works, although the latter was in early editions attributed to both writers. Fletcher himself said that Beaumont was attributed so-authorship of many works that belonged solely to Fletcher or to other collaborators.

One play in the canon, Sir John Van Olden Barnavelt, existed in manuscript and was not published till 1883.

www.ingramcontent.com/pod-product-compliance
Lightning Source LLC
Chambersburg PA
CBHW060129050426

42448CB00010B/2036